THE AMERICAN KENNEL CLUB'S
Meet the
Lab™

The Responsible Dog Owner's Handbook

AKC's Meet the Breeds Series

I-5
EST · 2013
·PRESS·
I-5 Publishing, LLC™

D1362152

Brought to you by The American Kennel Club and The Labrador Retriever Club.

Lead Editor: Lindsay Hanks
Art Director: Cindy Kassebaum
Production Coordinator: Leah Rosalez
Book Project Specialist: Karen Julian

I-5 PUBLISHING, LLC™
Chief Executive Officer: Mark Harris
Chief Financial Officer: Nicole Fabian
Vice President, Chief Content Officer: June Kikuchi
General Manager, I-5 Press: Christopher Reggio
Editorial Director, I-5 Press: Andrew DePrisco
Art Director, I-5 Press: Mary Ann Kahn
Digital General Manager: Melissa Kauffman
Production Director: Laurie Panaggio
Production Manager: Jessica Jaensch
Marketing Director: Lisa MacDonald

Photographs by The American Kennel Club: 119, 120; Blackhawk Productions (Dwight Dyke): Cover, 4, 21, 33, 34. 49, 51, 59, 62, 66-67, 71, 72, 75, 82-83, 86, 102-103, 104, 108, 110, 114, 118; Gina Cioli/I-5 Studio: Cover, Back Cover, 8, 10, 17, 29, 38, 42, 45, 50, 53, 63, 80, 94, 124; Close Encounters of the Furry Kind: 4, 26-27, 30, 43, 70, 73, 76, 78, 121; Diane Lewis Photography: Cover, 4, 9, 12, 13, 16, 17, 20, 23, 24, 28, 31, 36-37, 40, 46-47, 52, 56-57, 61, 69, 80, 81, 85, 91, 92-93, 99, 100, 101, 112-113, 116; Fox Hill Photo: Cover, 11, 25, 32, 35, 39, 54, 60, 64, 65, 68, 74. 79, 94, 87, 88, 89, 95, 96, 97, 98, 107, 117; Mark Raycroft Photography: 1, 3, 6-7, 14-15, 18-19, 22, 33, 48, 55, 58, 98, 111, 115; Noppadol Paothong: 41, 44, 105

Library of Congress Cataloging-in-Publication Data
The American Kennel Club's meet the lab : the responsible dog owner's handbook.
    p. cm. -- (AKC's meet the breeds)
Includes bibliographical references and index.
ISBN 978-1-935484-70-7
1. Labrador retriever. 2. Labrador retriever--Training. I. American Kennel Club.
SF429.L3A64 2011
636.752'7--dc23

                      2011016673

This book has been published with the intent to provide accurate and authoritative information in regard to the subject matter within. While every precaution has been taken in the preparation of this book, the author and publisher expressly disclaim any responsibility for any errors, omissions, or adverse effects arising from the use or application of the information contained herein. The techniques and suggestions are used at the reader's discretion and are not to be considered a substitute for veterinary care. If you suspect a medical problem, consult your veterinarian.

I-5 Publishing, LLC™
3 Burroughs, Irvine, CA 92618
www.facebook.com/i5press
www.i5publishing.com

Printed and bound in the United States
17 16 15 14   7 8 9 10

Meet Your New Dog

Welcome to *Meet the Lab*. Whether you're a long-time Lab owner, or you've just purchased your first puppy, we wish you a lifetime of happiness and enjoyment with your new pet.

In this book, you'll learn about the history of the breed; receive tips on feeding, grooming, and training; and learn about all the fun you can have with your dog. The American Kennel Club and I-5 Press hope that this book serves as a useful guide on the lifelong journey you'll take with your canine companion.

The Labrador Retriever is the most popular breed in the United States, in no small part due to the breed's aptitude to please, even temperament and trainability. Owned and cherished by millions across America, Labs thrive as part of an active family, make great sporting companions, and serve as dedicated assistance dogs, law enforcement K9s, and search and rescue dogs.

As a result of their versatility, Labs excel in many AKC events, including conformation (dog shows), obedience, rally, agility, tracking, hunt tests, field trials and more. Thousands of Labs have earned the AKC Canine Good Citizen certification by demonstrating their good manners at home and in the community. We hope that you and your Lab will become involved in AKC events, too! Learn how to get involved at www.akc.org/events or find a training club in your area by searching www.akc.org/events/training-clubs.cfm.

We also encourage you to connect with other Lab owners on the AKC website (www.akc.org), through our Facebook page (www.facebook.com/americankennelclub), and via Twitter (@akcdoglovers). Also visit The Labrador Club (www.thelabradorclub.com), the national parent club for the Labrador Retriever and an authority on the breed, to join the club and learn from reputable exhibitors and breeders.

Enjoy *Meet the Lab*!

Sincerely,

Dennis B. Sprung
AKC President and CEO

24

32

91

96

Contents

CHAPTER ONE

Do You Adore the Labrador?

If there is one thing Labrador Retrievers do best, it's retrieving. Labs love to fetch stuff and carry something—*anything*—in their mouths. You'll be amazed at the Lab's obsession with retrieving. If he's not carrying a bird, then sticks and socks will do. You can usually tell if a person owns a Lab by the number of sticks and branches piled up at his back door! So don't blame your Labrador when you can't find your shoes or the remote. He can't help it; that need to retrieve is in your dog's DNA.

It's in the Genes

What does it mean that retrieving is in a Lab's genes? In the early 1800s, an Earl in Newfoundland, Canada, bred a specific type of dog with long legs and short hair who was good at running and swimming. These qualities, in addition to a fun-loving and energetic personality, are perfect for retrieving.

Must Put in Mouth

Chewing goes hand-in-hand with retrieving, and Lab puppies are miniature chewing machines that often leave telltale marks on furniture and woodwork like handrails and baseboards. How can you stop your Lab from chewing? Provide lots of colorful chew toys and teach your Lab pup what he may and may not chew. You must closely watch your Labrador to train him *not* to chew, or you will end up with an adult Lab that continues to destroy your home!

The Lab is super friendly and will not be happy unless he can hang out with you. He loves being part of an active family that includes the dog in everyday activities. He enjoys fun outdoor games, which are the best way for him to channel his energy and enthusiasm. And Labradors are just as comfortable in the water as they are on land. Swimming is their favorite sport (after retrieving, of course).

A Labrador Retriever needs exercise, so take him on one or two long walks every day and spend some quality time with him. Exercise and time with you will keep your Lab from getting bored or lazy, which usually leads to your Lab destroying things!

Lab puppies are *very* energetic, so be careful when you're playing with and training your pup. Take lots of breaks, especially if you see your puppy getting too excited!

What to Expect

The Lab is an "easy keeper." His short coat requires little grooming and upkeep. But Labs shed twice a year and drop a little hair all year long. You'll find Lab hair on the floor, your clothes, the furniture—everywhere. Be prepared to vacuum regularly, but your best pal is worth the 15 minutes of vacuuming a week, right? Of course, he is!

Although the Lab excels in lots of doggy activities and competitions, he is known to want to do things his way. Labrador Retrievers are as strong-willed as they are eager to please, so there can be challenges in training. The best time to teach your Lab good doggy manners is when he's a puppy before he gets too big to handle!

Is a Lab Right for You?

Before you start calling Labrador breeders or rescue groups, your family should decide how a dog will fit into your lives and the kinds of activities you want to do with

Mr. Popularity

The Labrador Retriever has been the most popular dog in the United States for the past twenty years, according to the American Kennel Club. That's one popular dog! To register your Lab with the AKC, fill out the Dog Registration Application you received when you bought your puppy and simply mail it to the AKC in North Carolina or register online at www.akc.org.

AMERICAN KENNEL CLUB

Labs are high-energy dogs. If you get one, be prepared to spend a lot of outdoor time with him.

The Need to Retrieve

Your Lab wants to do the one thing he does best—retrieve! Try playing Frisbee at a local dog park or go to the beach and have your Lab play "catch" with his favorite tennis ball. And while you're enjoying the sun and surf, give your Lab a chance to roll in the sand and swim in the ocean. Your dog will love you for it! Always check the local ordinances regarding whether dogs are permitted on the beach or in the park before going.

Did You Know?

The movie *Marley & Me* required the casting of twenty-five different Labrador Retrievers to portray the naughty yellow Lab at different ages. Most of the dogs were used to film the puppy scenes.

You Must Commit, Too!

Getting a dog is exciting, but it's also a huge responsibility. That's why it's important to educate yourself on all that is involved in being a good pet owner. As a part of the Canine Good Citizen Test, the AKC has a "Responsible Dog Owner's Pledge," which states:

I will be responsible for my dog's health needs.

☐ I will provide routine veterinary care, including check-ups and vaccines.

☐ I will offer adequate nutrition through proper diet and clean water at all times.

☐ I will give daily exercise and regularly bathe and groom.

I will be responsible for my dog's safety.

☐ I will properly control my dog by providing fencing where appropriate, by not letting my dog run loose, and by using a leash in public.

☐ I will ensure that my dog has some form of identification when appropriate (which may include collar tags, tattoos, or microchip identification).

☐ I will provide adequate supervision when my dog and children are together.

I will not allow my dog to infringe on the rights of others.

☐ I will not allow my dog to run loose in the neighborhood.

☐ I will not allow my dog to be a nuisance to others by barking while in the yard, in a hotel room, etc.

☐ I will pick up and properly dispose of my dog's waste in all public areas, such as on the grounds of hotels, on sidewalks, in parks, etc.

☐ I will pick up and properly dispose of my dog's waste in wilderness areas, on hiking trails, on campgrounds, and in off-leash parks.

I will be responsible for my dog's quality of life.

☐ I understand that basic training is beneficial to all dogs.

☐ I will give my dog attention and playtime.

☐ I understand that owning a dog is a commitment in time and caring.

Labradors make great family pets. They are the most popular dog breed in America today.

Labradors are happiest when they get to stretch out their legs, run at top speed, and play in the water. Throw in another canine companion or two, and your dog will be in heaven.

him. If you want your dog to hunt and retrieve, look for a Labrador from field-bred parents. If you want to try to win blue ribbons at American Kennel Club dog shows with your Lab, then look for breeders who show their dogs and breed the ones that win awards. If you just want a fun and energetic pet, look for a healthy combination of energy and loyalty.

All puppies can be a handful, but a Labrador Retriever is extremely high-energy with a crazy zest for life that can be overwhelming, even for the most well-prepared family. Because the Lab is so popular, many people don't realize that, while highly trainable, these dogs require lots of training. Your Lab wants to please you; he just needs to learn how to do it. Puppy training programs and other obedience training can work wonders in transforming a "wild and crazy" Labrador into a well-behaved, happy canine good citizen.

Meet the Lab and More!

A great place to see Labradors and more than 200 other dog and cat breeds is at Meet the Breeds, hosted by the American Kennel Club and presented by Pet Partners, Inc. Not only can you see dogs, cats, puppies, and kittens of all sizes, you can also talk to experts in each of the breeds. Meet the Breeds features demonstration rings to watch events with law enforcement K9s, grooming, agility, and obedience. You also can browse the more than 100 vendor booths for every imaginable product for you and your pet.

It's great fun for the whole family. Meet the Breeds takes place in the fall in New York City. For more information, check out www.meetthebreeds.com.

A Big Decision

Getting a dog is a *huge* decision and should be based on what's best for you, your family, and the dog. Don't rush into it! Have lots of talks as a family about how a Lab will affect your lives and everyday activities. With the right preparation, you and your Labrador Retriever can live happily ever after.

At a Glance ...

The first thing that a Labrador Retriever owner must understand is the breed's need to chew. Providing chew toys, dog-proofing the home, and training your Lab for what *not* to chew are essential.

· ·

Labs love their people and need to be included with the family in all activities.

· ·

Great with kids, easy to groom, and super friendly, the Lab offers many wonderful pet qualities.

· ·

Labs can get a little crazy, especially as puppies! You must commit to a training program—this can make the difference between living with a great pet or a troublemaker.

· ·

Look beyond the breed's popularity to determine if a Labrador really is the right dog for you, and if you are right for a Lab!

CHAPTER TWO

Recipe for a Retriever

hy do all Labradors look the same? Have you noticed that a black Lab looks exactly like a yellow Lab or a chocolate Lab, except for the color? That is not an accident: it's what makes a purebred dog different from a mixed-breed dog.

This "sameness" from dog to dog is the special "type" that defines a breed, and the recipe for this type is called a breed standard. The breed standard is simply a written description of all of

Chocolate Labrador Retriever puppies have an allure all their own. Regardless of color, your Lab puppy should be healthy, alert and friendly.

a dog's body parts, including his head, legs, paws, and tail, and even his character and personality.

Not only do all Labradors look alike, but to a marked degree, they act alike, too. By definition, Labrador Retrievers are eager to please, kind, outgoing, and obedient. In other words, Labradors are designed to be family dogs! As the retriever part of their name indicates, they also make great hunters, able to retrieve ducks, geese, quail, and other game birds in the field.

Every dog breed registered by the American Kennel Club has a breed standard, a written description of the ideal specimen, which includes not only the

What is a Parent Club?

Breed standards are written by experienced breeders across the country who belong to that particular breed's parent club. The American Kennel Club then officially approves the standard. A parent club is a national organization recognized by the AKC that represents a particular dog breed. The Lab standard was written by the Labrador Retriever Club, Inc., which is the AKC parent club of the Labrador Retriever breed. You can learn more about the Labrador Retriever Club at its website, www.thelabradorclub.com.

AMERICAN KENNEL CLUB

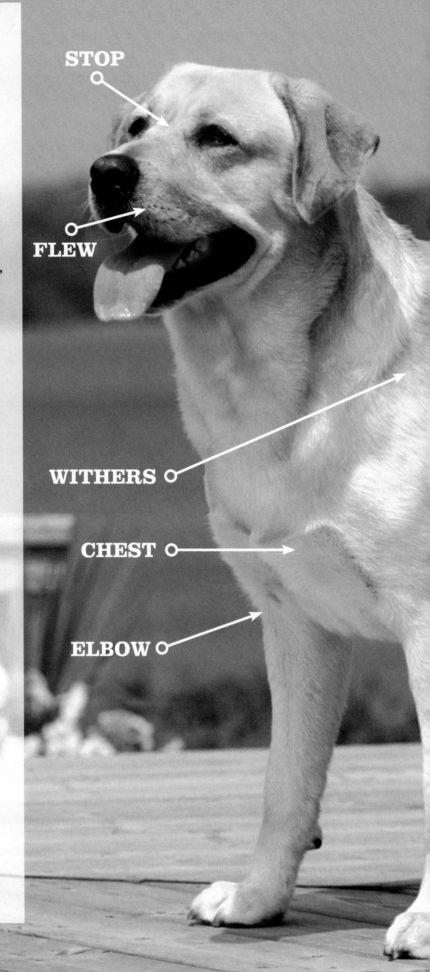

The Lab in Brief

COUNTRY OF ORIGIN:
Canada (Newfoundland province)

ORIGINAL USE:
Fisherman's working dog and waterfowl retriever.

GROUP:
Sporting

AVERAGE LIFE SPAN:
12 to 14 years

COAT:
Double-coated with a short, straight, dense outercoat, and a soft, water-resistant undercoat.

COLOR:
Solid black, yellow, or chocolate. Small white chest spot allowed, but not desired.

GROOMING:
Brush daily during twice-yearly periods of heavy shedding; otherwise, weekly. Bathe only when necessary (i.e., if coat smells). Clean ears and teeth, and check nails once a week.

HEIGHT/WEIGHT:
Males, 22½ to 24½ inches and 65 to 80 pounds; females, 21½ to 23½ inches and 55 to 70 pounds.

TRAINABILITY:
High

PERSONALITY:
Cheerful and outgoing, keen to please, active, and adaptable.

ACTIVITY LEVEL:
High, especially when young.

GOOD WITH OTHER PETS:
Yes, with proper socialization and introduction.

NATIONAL BREED CLUB:
Labrador Retriever Club; inquiry@thelabradorclub.com; www.thelabradorclub.com

RESCUE:
Labrador Retriever Club; rescue2@hotmail.com; www.thelabradorclub.com

STOP

FLEW

WITHERS

CHEST

ELBOW

Anatomy of a Lab

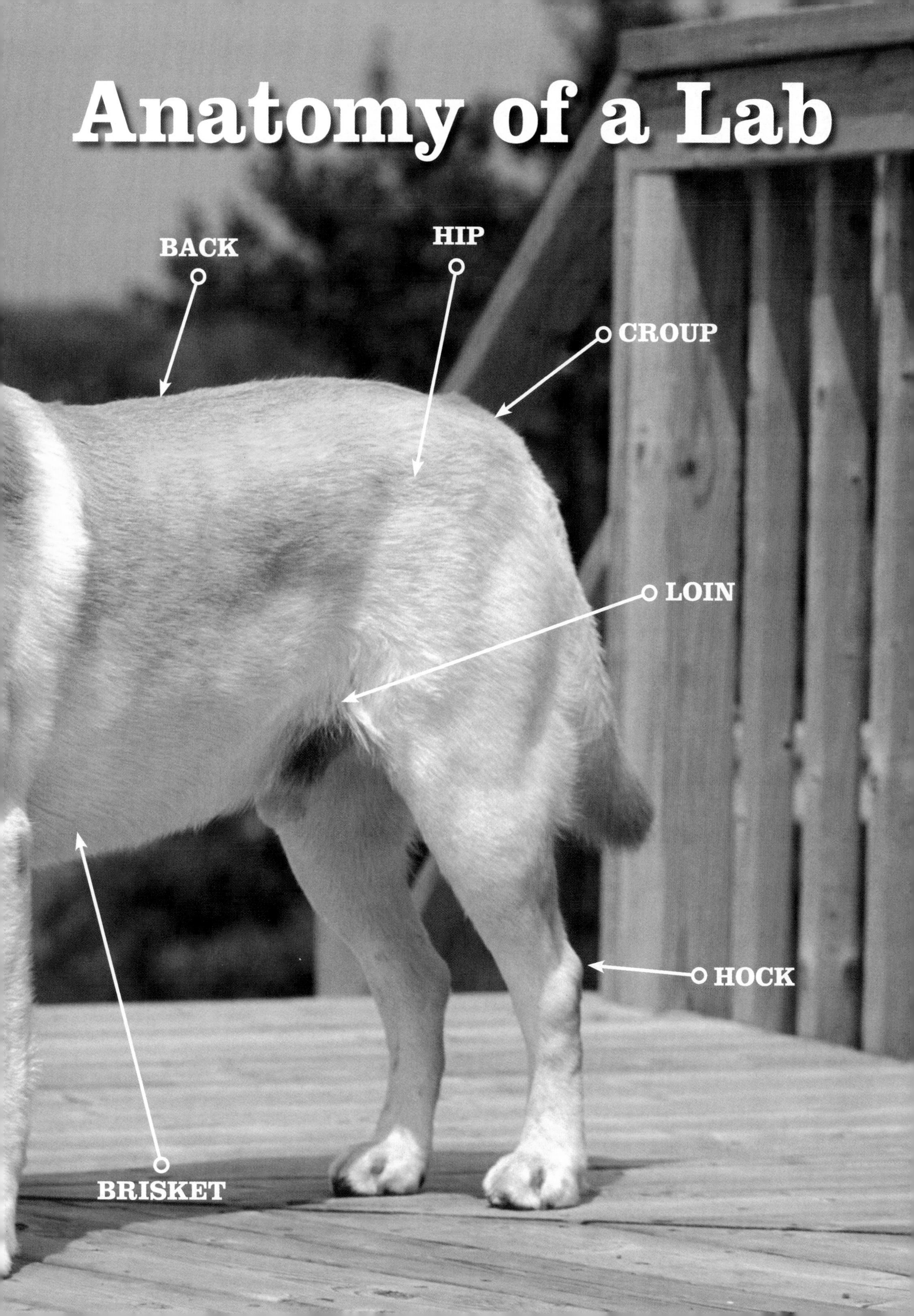

BACK

HIP

CROUP

LOIN

HOCK

BRISKET

physical traits but personality characteristics, too. That's why Labs look and act like Labs and Chihuahuas look and act like Chihuahuas.

So, who writes these standards anyway, and who uses them? Each dog breed has a national club called a parent club that protects and promotes the specific breed, and for Labs, the parent club is The Labrador Retriever Club (www.thelabradorclub.com), a member club of the American Kennel Club.

Every time a Labrador competes in a dog show, the judge uses the breed standard to decide how closely each Lab matches the breed standard. The judge will select as the winner the dog that conforms to the standard the best on that day.

That's why dogs that win ribbons at shows are bred—to continue a line of dogs that closely matches the breed standard. In fact, the true purpose of a dog show is to compare breeding stock. Breeders use the breed standard as the guideline to create the next generation of Labs.

For as long as people love Labrador Retrievers and the breed standard is used, Labs will be Labs forever!

Labradors were bred to retrieve, as the name reveals. Play a little catch with your dog every day, and he couldn't be happier.

What a Sport!

The Labrador Retriever isn't the only retriever. The AKC recognizes six retrievers in addition to the Labrador: the Chesapeake Bay Retriever, the Curly-Coated Retriever, the Flat-Coated Retriever, the Golden Retriever, and the Nova Scotia Duck Tolling Retriever. All of these retrievers belong to a group called the Sporting Group. This group of dogs includes all the hunting dogs—not just retrievers, but spaniels, setters, and pointing dogs, too.

A PIECE OF HISTORY

Originally from Newfoundland, Canada, Labrador Retrievers were initially used to work alongside fishermen, helping pull in nets and catch fish that escaped from fishing lines.

Throughout the breed's history, the Labrador Retriever has been drawn to the water and worked alongside people.

The AKC-accepted colors for Labradors are black, chocolate, and yellow (as shown here). Anything else you may find is not a true Labrador coloring.

Retrievers, like the Lab, retrieve downed prey (such as ducks, grouse, and pheasants) and return them to the hunter. Spaniels flush game out of dense brush, while setters and pointers find prey and either set (crouch) or point to them.

All Sporting breeds have lots of energy and are easily trainable. They need lots of exercise every day, so be sure to take your Lab out a couple of times every day for good, long walks. It's good for him and for you!

A Bona Fide Lab

The Labrador Retriever was bred in Newfoundland (a city near Labrador in Canada) as a hunting dog. Because of this, the Lab breed standard describes all the reasons that make the Lab perfect for hunting and retrieving.

A devoted dog with a strong back and long legs, Labs are medium-sized with lots of energy. The Lab has a short, thick, waterproof coat that comes in black, yellow, or chocolate. His muscular body is meant for long days of running and hunting. He has a straight, thick tail that he uses like an otter when he's swimming. He also has thick, powerful jaws for retrieving. Labs have great balance and can run through fields and backyards, easily dodging trees, and small hills. The dog is strong, and his body is thick. He should be in good shape, with a trim tummy. The average Labrador weighs 55 to 75 pounds.

Labrador Retrievers are widely known as fantastic pets for children. Their substantial size and docile temperament make them friendly and resilient.

The Labrador Retriever's body type and personality are perfect for a working dog in the country or a service dog in the city. He is easy to train, and he always wants to please his family. The Lab has a great personality with lots of excitement and happiness all rolled into one. His kind, friendly eyes show that he is gentle and very smart. Known for their easygoing and hardworking temperament, the Labrador Retriever truly is man's (or woman's, or kid's) best friend!

Does this sound like your Lab?

Black, Yellow, and Chocolate

AMERICAN
KENNEL CLUB

Though you may hear about silver Labs or white Labs, there are only three colors recognized by the American Kennel Club breed standard: black, yellow, and chocolate. Black Labs are all black. Yellow Labs can range from a reddish-orange to a light cream color. Chocolate Labs are dark brown with brown noses.

Labrador Breed Standard

AMERICAN KENNEL CLUB

OVERALL: The Labrador Retriever is a strongly built, medium-sized, short-coupled dog possessing a sound, athletic, well-balanced conformation. The most distinguishing characteristics of the Labrador Retriever are its short, dense, weather-resistant coat; an "otter" tail; a clean-cut head with broad back skull and moderate stop; powerful jaws; and its "kind," friendly eyes, expressing character, intelligence and good temperament.

PROPORTION: Length from the point of the shoulder to the point of the rump is equal to or slightly longer than the distance from the withers to the ground. The body must be of sufficient length to permit a straight, free and efficient stride; but the dog should never appear low and long or tall and leggy in outline.

HEAD: The skull should be wide, well developed but without exaggeration. There should be a moderate stop—the brow slightly pronounced so that the skull is not absolutely in a straight line with the nose. The nose should be wide and the nostrils well developed; black on black or yellow dogs, and brown on chocolates. The ears should hang moderately close to the head, set rather far back, and somewhat low on the skull, slightly above eye level. Kind, friendly eyes imparting good temperament, intelligence, and alertness are a hallmark of the breed. They should be of medium size, set well apart, and neither protruding nor deep set; brown color in black and yellow Labradors, and brown or hazel in chocolates.

NECK: The neck should be of proper length to allow the dog to retrieve game easily. It should be muscular and free from throatiness. The neck should rise strongly from the shoulders with a moderate arch.

TOPLINE: The back is strong and the topline is level from the withers to the croup when standing or moving. However, the loin should show evidence of flexibility for athletic endeavor.

TAIL: The tail is a distinguishing feature of the breed. It should be very thick at the base, gradually tapering toward the tip, of medium length, and extending no longer than to the hock; free from feathering and clothed thickly all around with the Labrador's short, dense coat, thus having that peculiar rounded appearance that has been described as the "otter" tail. The tail completes the balance of the Labrador by giving it a flowing line from the top of the head to the tip of the tail. It may be carried gaily, but should not curl over the back.

FOREQUARTERS: Forequarters should be muscular, well coordinated and balanced with the hindquarters. The shoulders are well laidback, long and sloping. When viewed from the front, the legs should be straight with good, strong bone. Viewed from the side, the elbows should be directly under the withers, and the front legs should be perpendicular to the ground and well under the body. Feet are strong and compact, with well-arched toes and well-developed pads.

HINDQUARTERS: The Labrador's hindquarters are broad, muscular and well developed from the hip to the hock with well-turned stifles and strong, short hocks. The hind legs are strongly boned, muscled with moderate angulation at the stifle, and powerful, clearly defined thighs. When the dog is standing, the rear toes are only slightly behind the point of the rump. Feet are strong and compact, with well-arched toes and well-developed pads.

—Excerpts from the Labrador Retriever Breed Standard

One in a Million

The Lab breed standard describes the ideal Labrador Retriever as a kind and energetic dog perfect for hunting and retrieving, but also as a great family dog with a heart of gold. By working with a breeder, you can find a Lab that adheres to the breed standard in appearance and temperament. The best pet Lab has both the good looks of a champion and the trainability and focus of a hunting dog.

But no matter what, be sure to choose a Lab that's right for you. All Labs, regardless of what they look like, love to swim, play, and retrieve. Your Lab will fetch sticks and Frisbees for as long and as far as you can throw them. Labrador Retrievers, in their natural excitement for life, can hardly help but to rip up your newspapers and magazines, jump on your bed, and lick you all over your face. Keeping your Lab happy and his behavior under control are a part of your responsibility as an owner. With the right training and rearing, your Lab will be the best and most loyal friend you will ever have.

An easy keeper with a fun-loving personality and a strong desire to please, the Labrador Retriever makes a great companion pet.

At a Glance ...

The Labrador Retriever breed standard describes the Lab as a hunter and a retriever. He loves to run, swim, and retrieve all day, every day!

· ·

The Lab is friendly, outgoing, and energetic; he is never aggressive or mean.

· ·

You should pick the Lab that is best for your family.

CHAPTER THREE

Finding the **Perfect Pet**

Once you decide that the Labrador Retriever is the best breed for you, it's time to actually go out and find one. Unfortunately, you can't just go to Labs 'R' Us and pick one up. You will have to do some homework first and be patient. Read up on the breed as much as you can—look at magazines, books, and websites. After you have researched the breed and decided that a Lab is the dog for you, then start looking for a reputable breeder. When you start interviewing breeders, you'll know what questions

Don't just bring home the first puppy you see. They're all adorable, but finding the right Lab for you will require time and research to learn the pup's temperament and personality, as well as his health condition.

to ask and have an idea of what traits to look for from the puppies you see. Familiarize yourself with the breed before you start shopping. It can sometimes take several months before you find the dog of your dreams.

Why the Wait?

A responsible breeder is a person who breeds only for the sake of the breed, not for money or for fun. To find a good, trustworthy breeder, spend a day at a dog show, a field trial, or another event sponsored by the American Kennel Club where you can meet Labrador people—breeders, owners, and handlers—and ask them questions about their dogs. Be polite: most dog people are more than happy to talk to people about their breed, but make sure you don't catch someone just as he is getting ready to enter the show ring or agility course. If you know someone who owns a great Lab, ask him where he got his dog and see if that breeder is the right one for you.

The AKC recognizes good breeders through its the Breeder of Merit program, enrolling dedicated breeders who continue to produce healthy, capable, and beautiful purebred dogs. Every breeder in the program must have at least five years of involvement with AKC events, must have earned no fewer than four

Paper Points

AMERICAN KENNEL CLUB

A responsible breeder will be able to provide your family with a pedigree and an American Kennel Club registration.

AKC REGISTRATION: When you buy a new Labrador Retriever puppy from a breeder, ask the breeder for an American Kennel Club Dog Registration Application form. The breeder will have filled out most of the application for you. When you fill out your portion of the document and mail it to the AKC, you will receive a Registration Certificate proving that your Lab is officially part of the AKC. Besides recording your name and your dog's name in the AKC database, registration helps fund good works such as canine health research, search-and-rescue teams, educating the public about responsible dog care, and much more.

CERTIFIED PEDIGREE: A pedigree is an AKC-approved certificate proving that your dog is a genuine Labrador Retriever. It is your puppy's family tree, showing the names of his parents and grandparents. If your dog is registered with the AKC, the organization will have a copy of your dog's pedigree on file, which you can order from its website (www.akc.org). Look for any titles that your Lab's ancestors have won, including any AKC dog shows, competitions, or certifications. This history proves that your Lab had healthy parents that followed the Labrador Retriever breed standard. A pedigree doesn't guarantee the health or good personality of a dog, but it's a starting point for picking out a good Lab puppy.

titles for dogs that he or she has bred or co-bred, must perform a necessary health screening as recommended by the parent club, and must be sure that all puppies bred are registered with the AKC. Visit the AKC website (www.akc.org) to view the names of the Breeders of Merit in your state. You can also look up breeders with AKC litters on the online breeder classified list.

If you are looking for a Labrador Retriever as a pet and not as a show dog, hunting companion, or competition dog, then you can rely on any Breeder of Merit or responsible breeder to lead you to the right puppy. If, on the other hand, you know that you want to show your puppy or train him for field or agility trials, then you need to find a qualified breeder who specializes in breeding show, field, or performance Labs.

Did You Know?

The Labrador Retriever's thick "otter-like" tail acts like a rudder and helps the dog swim. The tail should be very thick at the base and gradually taper toward the tip. Docking or altering the length or natural carriage of the tail is a disqualification, according to the breed standard.

The Labrador Retriever can be a great addition to any family willing to give the dog the attention he needs. Discuss the responsibilities involved in pet ownership with your family before you bring a new dog into the mix.

A Boy or a Girl!

Is a male or a female Labrador Retriever right for you and your family? Both male and female Labs are loving and loyal, but there are just a few physical differences between them.

The adult male Lab can be about 2 inches taller than the female and about 10 pounds heavier, weighing 65 to 80 pounds. Although males tend to be more even-tempered, they are more energetic and clumsy as they grow. They also can be very bossy and territorial with people and other dogs. The adult female Lab is lovable and easy to live with, but she can be a bit more moody. One day she is sweet and calm, then wild and getting into trouble the next.

All responsible owners who do not plan to breed their Labs should have their dogs spayed or neutered. Female dogs are spayed, and male dogs are neutered. Besides making your Lab better behaved, spaying or neutering has certain health benefits, such as reducing the chances of getting certain types of cancer. Spaying and neutering should be done by all pet Lab owners to help control the pet population.

For breeder contacts, you can also go to The Labrador Retriever Club, the national breed club. You can find extensive information about the Lab and a list of breeders on the club's website (www.thelabradorclub.com). If your family has any doubts about a breeder, feel free to ask for references from other families that have purchased puppies from them.

Breeder Selection

Once your family has found a few breeders who appear to be responsible and trustworthy, use the following steps to make sure that your hunch is correct.

STEP 1: Ask the Right Questions: To start, your family should call or e-mail each breeder and ask some basic questions. Ask them what AKC competitions they're involved in, such as showing, field trials, or other performance events or dog-related activities. Breeders usually choose the winners of these competitions to breed their next litter of puppies. If a breeder has no interest in dog sports, your family should probably keep looking.

Other good questions to ask include:

* Have long have you been breeding Labs? The longer, the better. More years means more experience.

* Have the puppies been raised in the home? Where? Puppies raised in the home are better socialized and can be looked after better and more often.

* Have you tested or evaluated your Labrador Retriever puppies for their temperaments? A good breeder makes sure his puppies are suitable for a new home.

* How often is the mother bred? Once a year is plenty. If it is more than that, you could be dealing with an indiscriminate breeder.

* Which colors of Labs do you have? There are only three acceptable colors: yellow, black, and chocolate. Breeders with "exotic" colors are trying to fool inexperienced dog owners to make more money. Avoid them.

* Can I get all of your warranties and guarantees in writing? Do you have a purchase contract? A good breeder won't have a problem putting his guarantees in writing. Don't just take his word for it.

* Will you take the dog back at any time, for any reason, if I cannot keep him? The answer to this question must be a resounding *yes*, which proves you are dealing with a breeder who really cares about his dogs.

STEP 2: Be Prepared to Answer Questions: Breeders will ask your family questions, too, about previous dogs you have owned, which breeds, and how you liked owning those dogs. They will want to know if you live in a house or an apartment, with or without a backyard and a fence, and whether or not there are any children or other pets in the house.

It's perfectly normal for breeders to ask you lots of questions; actually, you should be worried if they don't! A good breeder wants to know whether your family is right for his puppies and whether you will provide a good and loving home for whichever pup you choose.

Be ready to answer a variety of questions regarding your pet ownership background and reasons for interest in the Labrador Retriever breed specifically.

3, 2, 1… Contract!

Most breeders have a puppy sales contract that includes specific health guarantees and reasonable return policies. The breeder should agree to accept a puppy back if things don't work out. He also should be willing to check up on the Lab's progress after the pup leaves for his new home and should be available to help if you have questions or problems with the pup.

Worth Every Penny!

Healthy Labrador Retrievers with desirable breeder qualities will not be inexpensive. Many breeders will lower the high price of a Lab if he has qualities that will not be good for showing or breeding. This does not mean that he won't make a great pet. He should still be as healthy as any other puppy that the breeder sells, and he should look and act like a true Labrador Retriever. Don't look for a discount puppy. You will be glad that you spent the appropriate amount of money to buy a healthy, perfect pet Lab for you and your family.

When looking for a puppy to purchase, pick one that appears well socialized to people and other dogs. This will help speed up the socialization and training process once you bring him home.

Common questions you will encounter during the interview will include things such as:

- Have you previously owned a Labrador Retriever? The breeder is trying to gauge whether you are already familiar with the breed and its specific needs. If this is your first Lab, share the information you've learned from your research. This is where all your homework comes into play.

- How many hours are you away from home throughout the week? Labs need a lot of attention, especially when they're puppies. They can't just live in the backyard by themselves; they'll get sad and lonely! Reassure the breeder that you understand the time commitment involved and that you are excited and prepared for a Labrador's daily care.

- How long have you wanted a Labrador Retriever? Cautious breeders want to avoid impulse buyers. The breeder wants to hear that you have carefully thought out the decision before you bring a dog home.

STEP 3: Breeder Visit: If the initial interview went well, your family should set up an appointment to visit the breeder at his home. A responsible breeder will welcome a visit from your family to take a look around his home and property.

When you arrive, see whether the area and house are clean. All of the dogs should appear healthy (clean eyes, well groomed, trimmed toenails) and have fresh water and room to move and play. The breeder should also know every dog by name and each puppy as an individual.

You also should be able to meet the dam (mother) of the litter of puppies. Ask if the sire (father) is on the property, too. Sometimes, the father belongs to another person. This is perfectly normal. If that's the case, ask to see pictures of him. Pay special attention to both parents' temperaments and body types.

Do not visit one breeder after another without going home and showering and changing clothes, including your shoes. It's easy to transmit bacteria, parasites, and disease, and young puppies may not be strong enough to fight these dangers.

When you visit a breeder, keep an eye out for the following:

• A clean, well-maintained facility. There should be an overall impression of cleanliness, from the dogs themselves to the areas they eat, sleep, and play.

• No overwhelming odors. This could be a sign of neglect or illness among the dogs.

• Well-socialized dogs and puppies. Fearfulness and anxiety among the dogs are bad signs. The pups should be used to interacting with people and their littermates.

When you visit the breeder's home, look for a happy, healthy Labrador puppy to make your own. Whether he's show quality or not, you'll benefit from choosing a good representation of the breed, according to the breed standard.

Picking a Puppy

A visit to a breeder involves much more than puppy hugs and kisses—even though they are the best part of it! Think of it like an interview. You are looking for a new addition to your family, so you are looking for the best pup possible. Check out all the possibilities: the puppies, their parents, the breeder, and especially the living environment where the pups have grown up.

Watch how the puppies play with their littermates and respond to their surroundings, especially with new people. They should be active and outgoing. In most groups, some puppies will be more outgoing than others, but even a quiet pup should not be overly shy or shrink away from your touch.

Breeders should point out the different personalities in their puppies. The breeders have spent the past seven or eight weeks cuddling and caring for the Labrador Retriever puppies, and they should know the different habits and temperaments of each one. Breeders' advice can help you pick out the best puppy for you and your family.

It's easy to want the first puppy you see. First and foremost, you want a healthy puppy that is energetic and loving. When you are picking out a puppy, be sure to look for these key things:

• The eyes should be clear and shiny, not crusted and cloudy.

• The inside of the ears should smell clean and shouldn't be red or swollen.

• The nose should be moist, but not runny.

• The tummy can be round, but not swollen or potbellied.

- The skin and coat should be soft and shiny, with no rashes or missing hair.
- Puppies should be active and playful, not scared, when you reach down to pet them.

Get the Goods

Make sure the breeder you decide to work with has all of the essential items to go with the puppy of your choice. When you purchase a pup from a breeder, you should receive the following:

Contract: Make sure you receive a copy of the purchase contract that you signed when you bought the puppy from the breeder. The contract should denote the puppy's purchase price, health guarantee, spay/neuter requirements, and conditions for returning the pup if necessary.

Health records: You should receive paperwork for all veterinary visits and immunizations for your puppy, as well as documentation for his date of birth. This will come in very handy when you take your dog for his first visit with your veterinarian of choice, within a few days of you bringing him home. These records will become part of your dog's permanent health file.

Pedigree: This is a copy of your puppy's family tree, listing your Lab's parentage as far back as possible, depending on how many generations the pedigree includes. It also lists any degrees and/or titles that those relatives earned. The price of the puppy is usually higher in championship lineages.

Registration papers: If the puppy's parents were registered with the AKC, the breeder should supply you with an application form to register your puppy with the organization, as well. At the least, you should receive a signed bill of sale that you can use to register the puppy yourself. A bill of sale's information will include the puppy's breed, birth date, sex, registered names of the parents, litter number, breeder's name, date of the sale, and the seller's signature. You must register your puppy if you want to compete in any AKC-sanctioned events.

General care kit: These items may vary, but the kit should include things like basic puppy care information, a small sample of the food your puppy has been eating while living with the breeder, and a blanket with the scent of his mother and littermates. A change in diet can upset an already anxious puppy's digestive system, so make any change to his diet gradually. And keep the blanket in the puppy's crate or resting area, to make your home feel and smell more familiar to your new puppy.

The Final Vote

A good breeder does more than just breed cute puppies. He will also help your family pick out the best puppy for your household. If you're very serious about showing or competing with your Labrador, be sure to tell the breeder about these intentions so that he will sell you the best possible dog for that endeavor. Of course, in the end, it's your family's decision. However, keep in mind that the breeder will be best able to pick the puppy that will fit your household. He's been with the litter from day one, so he knows more about the pups at this stage of their lives. Listen to him, and you'll be happy!

When you go to visit a Labrador breeder's puppies, pay attention to how they play and interact with you, your family, and the other dogs around them.

A well-socialized Lab will love spending time indoors and outdoors with you. Take time to pick out the right Lab puppy for your lifestyle.

At a Glance ...

With a popular breed like the Labrador Retriever, there are many breeders who are only interested in making money and who do not care about the health and wellness of their puppies. You must find an experienced breeder who is kind and loving and who truly cares about his puppies.

Ask lots of questions. You want to buy your Lab puppy from someone you can trust.

The Labrador Retriever Club, Inc. (www.thelabradorclub.com) is a trusted place to find a breeder. Membership in this AKC-affiliated club shows that a breeder is committed to following the breed standards set forth by the club.

Visiting the breeder allows you to see where the puppies have been raised, meet the puppies' parents, and make sure that all of the puppies are healthy.

Do you want a male or a female dog? Do you want a yellow Lab, a black Lab, or a chocolate Lab? Do you want to campaign your puppy as a show dog or a field trial contender? Be sure to tell your breeder these things so that he can help you select the right puppy.

Be sure to get all of the paperwork that you need from the breeder, such as pedigree, registration, health certificates, and the sales contract for your new puppy.

CHAPTER FOUR

Welcome Home, Lab!

It's almost the big day! You've chosen the perfect Labrador Retriever puppy, and you're counting down the days until you can bring him home. Before you do, your family should go shopping and buy some essential puppy supplies, then schedule time to puppy-proof your home. That's right, your family has to make sure that the house—indoors and out—is safe for the new puppy. And you have to make sure your house is safe *from* the puppy, too; cute as they are, puppies can be

Stock up on essential supplies before you bring your new puppy home. Such items include food and dishes, leash and collar, ID tags, gates, and bedding.

destructive machines. It's important to have your house ready before your Labrador comes home because you won't have much time after he arrives!

The Shopping List

Shopping for puppy supplies is a lot of fun, but it can get expensive, so start with the basics.

Food and water bowls: Buy two bowls, one for food and one for water. Stainless steel or ceramic ones are your best bet because they are lightweight, chew-proof, and easy to clean. Plastics can retain bacterial microorganisms more easily, and some dogs develop plastic allergies, so some veterinarians recommend avoiding plastic bowls altogether. Look for tip-proof bowls, too, because most puppies love to splash around in their water bowls. Your water-loving Lab definitely will!

Puppy food: Your Lab should eat quality puppy food that is specially made for his age and size. Most dog foods have unique formulas for dogs of different sizes. Your Labrador Retriever is considered a large dog, so he should eat large-breed food made for growing puppies. After a year old, he can switch to large-breed food for adult dogs. Your breeder probably told you what dog food your puppy is used to eating, and he may have given you a couple of days' worth of food. It's a good idea to keep your Lab on the same food he's been eating to avoid an upset tummy—after all, he will have more than enough changes to deal with. If you decide to change food brands, do so gradually over a few weeks by mixing more of the new with the old each day until only the new food is in his bowl.

Microchip Your Dog!

In addition to a dog collar, you should also think about having your vet or breeder insert a microchip in your dog to help find him if he ever gets lost. The microchip, when scanned, will show your dog's unique microchip number so that your Labrador Retriever can be returned to you as soon as possible. Go to www.akccar.org to learn more about the American Kennel Club's Companion Animal Recovery (AKC CAR) microchip identification system. Since 1995, the AKC has offered the AKC CAR program to responsible pet owners, and this 24/7 recovery service has been selected by millions of dog owners who are grateful for the peace of mind and service that AKC CAR offers.

Crate: A crate is the best tool for house-training your puppy, and it will become his favorite place to feel safe and protected. Think of it as your Lab's special den. Crates come in different sizes, designs, and colors and are made of wire, fabric, or plastic. Whichever crate you choose, be sure to buy one that your Labrador can grow into. In other words, get a crate for an adult Lab. While your puppy is small, block off portions of the crate so he doesn't poop or pee in one end and sleep in the other. As your puppy grows, give him more room in the crate.

Collar and ID tag: Your Labrador should have a collar that can expand to fit him as he grows. Lightweight, adjustable collars work best for both pups and adult dogs. Put the collar on as soon as your Lab comes home so he can get used to wearing it. The ID tag should have your dog's name and your phone number clearly displayed. Microchips and tattoos are additional identification options. But, by far, the collar is the fastest and most likely tool to help a good neighbor return your dog if he ever gets lost.

Leashes: Your family should buy two kinds of leashes: a thin, six-foot leather or nylon leash and an extendable leash that lengthens and retracts with the push of a button. The shorter leash is best for house-training and teaching your puppy obedience lessons. The extendable leash is great to use when you are taking your Labrador Retriever for a run. You can buy both types of leashes in an assortment of lengths and strengths depending on the size of your dog. For a Lab, longer is better to give him the opportunity to run around and check out the good

Beware the String!

Some less obvious items that can hurt your puppy are dental floss, yarn, needles and thread, and other stringy stuff. Puppies exploring the house at ground level will find and swallow the tiniest of objects and can end up in surgery. Most veterinarians will gladly tell you stories about the strange stuff they have removed from puppies' tummies.

Select a collar or halter for your puppy that fits him properly. Acclimating your new Labrador to the leash can take a little patience and good humor.

sniffing areas while still being near you. It's a good idea to teach your puppy how to heel (walk beside you without pulling on the leash) before you use the extendable leash so that he doesn't get used to running too far from you on walks. (See Chapter 7 for further training advice).

Gates: Baby gates are great to keep your puppy contained in certain parts or rooms of the house. It's a good idea to keep your puppy in a tiled or uncarpeted room or space that has a door to the backyard for potty trips. It's much more difficult to clean potty accidents on carpeting, so avoid putting your pup in carpeted areas as much as possible. By keeping your puppy in a safe place where he can't get into trouble, you are helping him learn rules without causing too many problems around the house.

However, just because your puppy is restricted to a certain area of the house doesn't mean you can ignore him! Labradors get bored very easily (just like we do), and they have been known to entertain themselves by chewing through doors and walls. If you have to leave your puppy alone, put him in his crate.

Bedding: Dog beds are just plain fun. They come in all shapes, sizes, and colors, but your dog just needs one that is soft and large enough for him to stretch out on. Don't go crazy and get the coolest, most expensive bed around. It's better to save your money until your Lab is older and less likely to chew up the fancy bed or get it dirty. For puppy bedding, use a large towel or blanket that can be washed easily (because it will need to be washed a lot!). If your pup will be sleeping in a crate, add a crate pad and the blanket inside. Be sure to replace the padding and blanket as they become tattered. Check for any loose threads that your puppy's nails or teeth could get caught on, because he is sure to play and chew on his bedding often.

It's better to provide your Lab with his own bed than to let him share yours. He'll take up a lot of space as he grows, and he'll appreciate having a place of his own to relax.

Grooming tools: Labradors almost always look good. A typical Lab will need baths only once or twice a month. So, find a pet shampoo you like because it will probably last you for a while. You don't need many types of combs to keep Labs clean and brushed. All you need is a slicker brush or a grooming glove to keep your dog's coat shiny. Introduce your puppy to grooming with a soft-bristle brush so he learns to enjoy grooming time. It also will get your pup used to being handled, which will help when it's time to clean his teeth or clip his nails. For those necessary pedicures, you'll need pet-specific nail clippers. Don't try to use your own for the job. You can go high-tech or low; some clippers are even equipped with sensors to detect where the nail's quick is, to avoid cutting too short and making your dog bleed.

Your Lab's adorable face needs regular grooming upkeep, too. Those floppy ears can easily trap bacteria, especially after a romp in the water. Get an ear-cleaning solution for such occasions, and check his ears often to determine when he needs an application. Dental cleaning from an early age will help fight oral disease later in his life. Human-grade toothpaste is harmful to dogs, but you can get special toothpaste and brushes for dogs. The younger he is when you start brushing, the more tolerant of it he'll be as he grows.

Toys: Puppies love to chew, so they need toys that are safe to gnaw and chew. If you don't give him toys to chew on, he'll decide that your shoes or furniture will do just fine. Old shoes, socks, or slippers are off limits because even the smartest puppy can't tell the difference between his belongings and yours. Retrieving toys like balls are a must for Labs because two of the breed's favorite hobbies are fetching and carrying things. Labradors also love all sorts of fuzzy toys that they can fetch and carry around. Many pups will even snuggle with their favorite toys when they sleep. But remember, as soon as your puppy shreds his fuzzy toys, throw them away. You don't want your puppy to swallow any of the fuzz or choke on button eyes or plastic squeakers.

Baby gates make excellent tools for keeping your pup contained in the rooms he's allowed to be in. It's much easier to puppy-proof a small area than an entire house.

A PIECE OF HISTORY

A Lab by any other name is still just as sweet. Before the breed arrived in Britain (gaining popularity and a new name after a vigorous breeding program), the Labrador Retriever's foundational breed was known as "St. John's Water Dog" and the "Lesser Newfoundland." People first started calling the breed "Labrador" in the late 1880s.

Toy Tip

Only offer two or three toys to your puppy at a time. If you give your Labrador too many toys, he'll get bored with all of them and get into trouble around the house. Only give him a few toys at a time and rotate them often. Each week, he will be excited to play with something new!

Cleaning supplies: These items are not for your dog but for you. You need to arm yourself with the right cleaning supplies before you bring your new puppy home. Until your Lab is house-trained, chances are you'll be cleaning up a lot of accidents. Keep lots of old rags, towels, and newspapers on hand for fast cleanup. And you'll need to invest in a strong enzymatic cleaner to remove any traces of urine that will otherwise draw your dog to the scene of the crime to pee again. It's instinct, so he won't be able to avoid it without your help.

Miscellaneous items: There are many other odds and ends that are great to have when you first bring home your new puppy. Puppy pee pads can be a helpful potty-training tool while your Labrador is learning where and when it's appropriate for him to go to the bathroom. They're also helpful for pet owners who might not be able to go home to let their puppies outside during the work-day. And while you're training your puppy, you'll want to keep some yummy treats on hand. There are many treat varieties available; just be sure to get something small enough for your Lab pup to digest (or easy for you to break into pieces). Save the treats for special occasions, or you'll spoil his diet! And if you find that your positive-reinforcement training needs a little help to curb your puppy's teething frenzy, bitter apple-flavored sprays exist to aid in dogs' chewing-behavior modification.

Puppy-Proofing Procedures

Labrador Retriever puppies are naturally curious and will investigate every-thing—and then they will try to destroy it! That's why puppy-proofing your house is a must. If you don't, you will regret it—and so will your house!

Adding a puppy to your home is a big change for the whole family. Make sure everyone in the household knows and follows the rules you'll be setting for the puppy.

You'll be amazed at what your puppy will find around your home. That's why it's important to *never* let your puppy roam around your house unsupervised.

Check your house for the following items that could be dangerous for your puppy, and place them out of his reach. The kitchen garbage can is a natural puppy magnet. Remember that your dog's nose is about 50,000 times more sensitive than yours. Just imagine how yummy these gross things smell to your new Labrador puppy! Collect all medicine bottles, cleaning materials, and bug sprays from around the house and lock them up in a cabinet that your puppy can't get into. Beware of fertilizers in your backyard and chemicals for cars like antifreeze and oil. These things are extremely toxic to your dog!

Electrical cords and wires pose danger to puppies, too; it's common for young dogs to get shocked when they chew on cords and wires! Safely bundle up all electrical cords and hide them behind specially made covers.

Another area you must puppy-proof is your bedroom. Pick up clothes, books and important papers off the floor and put them in your hamper, in the closet, or on your desk—out of your Lab's reach. Don't forget to close your closet doors. Puppies love all of these things because they smell like their favorite person—you!

Puppy-proofing is a never-ending chore. Your curious and "nosy" Lab will find his way into spaces that you thought he could never get into. You must always be a few steps ahead of him. Use common sense, and you and your Labrador puppy will enjoy a happy and safe home life together.

Socialization Equals Success!

Socialization is the most important part of a puppy's introduction to the human world. Although Labrador Retrievers are naturally outgoing and friendly, it is important to introduce them to strangers and new experiences at an early age. Pups that aren't socialized grow up to be scared and fearful of people and strange places. Some may become aggressive because of their fear and end up biting other dogs, strangers, or even you. Puppy socialization is the key to avoiding this and helping your dog grow into a friendly, well-trained adult Labrador Retriever.

The best time to socialize your dog is during his first twenty weeks of life. A good breeder will start the puppy's socialization process as soon as he's born. Hopefully, the breeder will handle the puppy often, petting him and giving him lots of love—sometimes bringing in different types of people of all ages to do the same. Litters raised around the hustle and bustle of routine life will become accustomed to the common sights, sounds, and smells around the house. Vacuum cleaners, coffee grinders, cars, and other noises can be frightening when puppies encounter them for the first time.

Doggy manners and socialization begin with the puppy's littermates. Puppies learn from their siblings how to interact appropriately with other dogs.

Once your Lab leaves the safety of his mother and littermates at eight to ten weeks, it's your job to continue his socialization training. Start with a quiet house for the first few days, letting him get used to his new environment, then slowly introduce him to the sights and sounds of his new world. Visit new places (dog friendly, of course) like parks or even the local grocery-store parking lot where there are crowds of people. Take him to the pet store and pet-friendly restaurants. Introduce him to people from all walks of life: adults and children, males and females, people in uniforms, people in wheelchairs, people with beards and mustaches, and all different ethnicities.

Familiarize your puppy to as many new situations and people as you can, so he won't be afraid of the encounter later in life. Set a goal to visit two new places a week for the next few months. Keep all of these situations upbeat and positive, which will teach your puppy that new experiences are happy and exciting.

While he's still young, take your Lab to puppy school. Some classes accept pups from ten to twelve weeks of age, as long as your puppy has had all of his shots. The younger the pup, the easier it is to train him. A good puppy class will teach good behavior rather than just obedience skills. Your puppy will be able to meet and play with other young dogs, and you will learn what tools you will need to train your puppy. Peer interaction is important to help to avoid or diminish any fear or anxiety your pup might have toward other dogs. Consistency and posititivity are key in early socialization and training.

Puppy classes are important not just for your dog but for you—especially if this is your first dog. Be a smart Labrador owner and continue with your dog studies and take more advanced training classes together as your dog gets older. Just like you, your puppy needs all the education he can get!

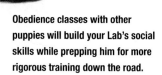

Obedience classes with other puppies will build your Lab's social skills while prepping him for more rigorous training down the road.

At a Glance ...

Be sure your family buys all of the necessary puppy supplies *before* bringing your new dog home. It's especially important to get safe chew toys for your new puppy.

Before the pup comes home, every family member should help to thoroughly puppy-proof the home and yard to create a safe environment for your Labrador Retriever. Puppy-proofing protects both your puppy and your house!

Once your pup is used to his new home, begin to introduce him to the human world around him. Socialize your Labrador by introducing him to new people and providing opportunities for him to interact with other dogs. Socialization is important for him to grow up friendly and confident.

CHAPTER FIVE

Training Your Lab Puppy

The Labrador Retriever is America's favorite breed for a good reason. Labs are smart, energetic, and easy to train. But don't think that all Lab puppies are born perfect! You will need to start training your pup as soon as possible. He won't learn everything all by himself. You will need to teach him how to behave in your house and around people. It's important to start training your Labrador early—the day you bring him home.

The Leader of the Pack

All dogs need someone to lead them. Your Labrador's first boss was his dam (mother), who watched over him and his brothers and sisters when he was first born. When he played too rough, his littermates cried and stopped the game. When he got too pushy, his mom shook him gently by the scruff of the neck.

Remember that human rules don't make sense to your puppy. You need to lead your puppy and help him understand what's right and wrong. This isn't easy, but it will strengthen your relationship with your pup.

The first five months of your Lab's life are the most important learning time for him. His mind is able to absorb more training lessons than at any other time in his life. You must fill this part of your puppy's life with positive training and introduce him to different types of people and places. This is called socialization, and it will help your puppy grow into a well-behaved, friendly dog. Socialization shows your puppy that strangers and new places aren't scary or dangerous.

Rewarding and Correcting

Humans like being rewarded for good behavior. Consider when you've finished a job before the deadline or bought the perfect present for a friend or a spouse.

Train your puppy on a leash in a quiet area where he can focus without being distracted by things around him. Use positive reinforcement tools such as toys and treats.

You appreciate your boss saying you've done a good job or receiving a big smile and hug from your loved one. All this extra, positive attention makes you want to do it again, right?

It's the same for your Labrador Retriever. Dogs' behavior tells us that anything a dog does that is rewarded will be repeated. This is called positive reinforcement. If something good happens when a dog does something, like receiving a tasty treat or hugs and kisses, he will want to do it again. So be sure to have lots of dog treats in your pockets when training your Lab. The easiest way to let your pup know he did something right is to give him a treat!

But what do you do when your dog does something wrong? Try to use the same training idea, but instead of a treat, correct the dog by saying a word like "no" in a calm voice and moving him away from what he is doing wrong. It is important to catch your dog while he is doing something wrong because, if you correct him later, he won't understand what he did wrong.

Training Keys

There are a few things that you need to know before you start training your Lab. Remember that you need to be your Lab's leader. Let him know that you are the boss. Be sure to teach him in a way that he will understand (sorry, barking just won't do it). Your puppy doesn't understand human rules, so be patient! It will take time for your Labrador Retriever to understand you—and for you to understand your Lab!

Say It Again and Again: Use the same word or command for each behavior every time you teach it, adding treats and lots of verbal praise such

Begin your puppy's training as soon as you bring him home, and make sure everyone in the household follows it consistently. A well-trained pup makes for a well-behaved adult—something everyone will appreciate.

Did You Know?

Labrador Retrievers are popular guide and rescue dogs. The breed's easy trainability and genial demeanor make for a reliable and loyal service companion.

as "Good dog!" and clapping to let your puppy know when he does something correctly. After a few times, your Labrador will understand and will be excited to repeat the behavior when he hears that same training word. For example, when teaching your pup to go potty outside, use the same potty words ("Go potty," "Get busy," or "Hurry up") each time he goes, adding the praise "Good boy!" when he's done. Your Lab will soon learn the correct reasons for those trips outside.

Five-Second Rule: Timing is very important when training your puppy. You have to catch him at the exact moment he is doing something good or bad to teach him whether something is right or wrong. If you correct your Lab more than five seconds after he's done something wrong, he won't understand why he is in trouble. So be sure to stay close to your Lab and watch him carefully! You want to be ready to train him the moment he does anything good or bad.

Training Tips

Successful puppy training depends on several important principles:

1. Use simple one-word commands and say them only once. Otherwise, your Labrador will learn that "Come" (or "Sit" or "Down") is a three- or four-word command.

2. Never correct your dog for something he did minutes earlier. Remember the five-second rule.

3. Always praise (and offer a treat) as soon as he does something good (or when he stops doing something bad). How else will your Lab know he's a good dog?

4. Be consistent. You can't jump on the bed together today, but then tell him it's wrong to jump on the bed tomorrow.

5. Never call your dog to you to correct him. He won't want to come when called because he thinks he'll get in trouble! Always go to your Lab to correct bad behavior, but be sure you catch him while he is doing something wrong or he won't understand why he is in trouble.

6. Never hit your dog as punishment. This will make your dog afraid of you, and he may react by growling or biting. Be sure to only use your voice to correct your Labrador Retriever, and keep your paws to yourself!

7. When you are rewarding your dog or correcting him, be sure to let your voice do the talking. Use a light, happy voice when your Lab does something good and a calm, firm voice when your Lab does something wrong. Remember that your dog doesn't speak English, but he can understand the tone of your voice.

Puppy Games

Playing games with your puppy is a great way to entertain your Labrador, while teaching him lessons at the same time. Keep your games short and your pockets full of treats, or else you will lose your Lab's attention. Then once you notice his attention wandering elsewhere, end the training session with something you already know he can do so that the lesson ends on a positive note.

Here are just a few games that are perfect for Labrador Retriever puppies. Your dog will have so much fun playing these games that he won't realize that he's learning a lesson.

Find Your Toy: Start by putting one of his favorite toys in the middle of the room. Ask your Lab, "Where's your toy?" and let him take it. Repeat this a few times. Then place your Lab outside the room and hide the toy where only part of it shows. Bring him back and again ask, "Where's your toy?" Clap and get excited when he finds it. Repeat this a few times. Finally, hide the toy completely and let your Lab sniff it out. Trust his nose...he will find his toy.

Because Labrador Retrievers are strong dogs, it's important to train your Lab to walk politely on leash. Otherwise, your walks can easily turn into tug-of-war sessions.

Doggy Day Care

If your family is very busy and no one is home during the day to keep him company, your Labrador Retriever will get pretty bored. If this sounds like your family's weekly routine, you may want to enroll your Lab puppy in doggy day care. There are many doggy day cares popping up all over the country, and they are a great way to help care for your Labrador Retriever while you are away from the house all day. Once you find a day care near you, search online at www.dog channel.com for tips on interview questions to ask and signs of a good facility to look for.

Be the Head Honcho

Wild dogs live in groups called "packs." In these packs, one dog acts as the leader and all the other dogs follow him and learn from him. Though your Labrador Retriever isn't wild, he still needs to have a leader. By training your dog when he is a puppy, he will learn from you as he would from his pack leader.

Use toys, praise, treats, and other positive-reinforcement tricks when training your pup. It's far more effective than scolding and using negative reinforcement.

Puppy Retrieve: This game helps teach the *come* command. With two people sitting on the floor about 10 or 15 feet apart, one person holds and pets the pup while the other calls to him "Puppy, puppy, come!" in a happy voice. When the pup comes running, give him big hugs and a tasty treat. Repeat back and forth several times, but don't overdo it. You can add a ball or toy and toss it back and forth for the puppy to retrieve. When he picks it up, praise and hug him some more, give him a treat to let go of the toy, then toss it back to the other person.

Where am I?: Play this game outdoors in your backyard or in another safe area. When your Lab is distracted, hide behind a tree or bush. Shout out "Where am I?" Peek out to see when he discovers you are gone and comes running back to find you. As soon as he gets close, come out, bend down with your arms spread out and call out his name. This game also teaches your puppy to come when called and helps teach the puppy to trust and depend on you.

Clicker Training

The clicker method of positive-reinforcement training has fast become popular among dog trainers and pet owners alike. It has been widely used by animal trainers for decades and been made more available to the general public in recent years with the arrival of many clicker training-related products on pet store shelves.

In clicker training, the trainer uses a tool called the "clicker," typically a small plastic box with a metal tongue that makes a clicking sound when it is

Is Your Puppy a S.T.A.R.?

The American Kennel Club has a great program for new puppy owners called the S.T.A.R. Puppy Program, which is dedicated to rewarding puppies that get off to a good start by completing a basic training class. S.T.A.R. stands for: Socialization, Training, Activity, and Responsibility.

You must enroll in a six-week puppy training course with an AKC-approved evaluator. When the class is finished, the evaluator will test your puppy on all the training taught during the course, such as being free of aggression toward people and other puppies in the class, tolerating a collar or body harness, allowing his owner to take away a treat or toy, and sitting and coming on command.

If your puppy passes the test, he will receive a certificate and a medal. You and your puppy will also be listed in the AKC S.T.A.R. Puppy records. To learn more about the AKC S.T.A.R. Puppy Program or to find an approved evaluator near you, check out www.akc.org/starpuppy.

SOCIALIZATION ★ TRAINING ★ ACTIVITY ★ RESPONSIBILITY

There are resources available to help you find a great trainer. Check with the AKC, the breed parent club, your veterinarian, and online for the right person.

pressed. This click sound is used to mark the exact instant of a rewardable behavior, which the trainer then follows with an immediate reward such as praise or a small treat. The closer the reward happens in time to the behavior, the faster the pup makes the connection and understands what he must do to earn another reward. Labs are very responsive to positive training techniques. Anyone can clicker train following these simple guidelines.

You begin by *charging* the clicker, teaching your dog that a reward is coming every time he hears the *marker* sound. Click

Finding a Good Trainer

Here are suggestions for finding training professionals who are compatible with your philosophies and needs:

• **Be clear about the kind of training you want for your dog.** It helps to know this ahead of time, before you start shopping for trainers. Read training books and research online. Choose the philosophies that meet your needs.

• **Locate trainers in your area.** Look online and ask your dog-owning friends, veterinarian, and breeder for any referrals. The Association of Pet Dog Trainers promotes dog-friendly training methods, and many of the organization's members are postive-method trainers. You can find a list of APDT member trainers in your area by searching their site, www.apdt.com.

• **Interview potential trainers that you're interested in.** Be certain that their techniques, training methods, and services offered meet your training goals.

• **Observe a class.** If a potential trainer says no to this request, then move on to someone else. Watch the trainer at work to be sure you are comfortable with the training methods and style used.

• **Ask for references.** Contact past students to find out about their experiences in class.

• **Select the trainer you are most comfortable with and sign up!** Keep in mind that you can leave and go to another trainer at any time, if you become uncomfortable or disagree with anything the trainer does. Your Labrador's safety and well-being are the most important factors.

and treat about a dozen times in rapid succession. At this point, the goal is to simply teach your puppy to associate the clicking noise with the treat. You'll know the clicker is charged when you see your Lab's eyes light up when he hears the click, then looks to you for a reward. You can use other markers besides the clicker, as well, such as a tongue cluck or a short and distinct marker word.

Now you're ready to apply the charged clicker's usefulness as a tool in whatever you want to train your dog to do. For instance, lure your puppy into a sit position. Say "Sit" and click the clicker just as your Lab's hind end hits the floor. Then immediately give him a treat. Repeat this multiple times in a row, and your well-trained puppy will soon know just what to do the moment you tell him to "Sit." For more extensive training information, read chapter 7 on "Basic Training Boot Camp."

A mother Lab's training can only go so far. Then it's up to you to help your pup reach his full, obedient potential.

At a Glance ...

The Labrador Retriever is a bright and eager puppy that will learn best if you act like a pack leader.

Be sure to start training your puppy during his first 20 weeks. This is when he can learn the most and the fastest.

Be consistent in your commands and in teaching your pup right from wrong.

Timing is important. You must catch your Labrador in the act to praise or correct his behavior.

Use games to lead up to training in a fun way.

If everyone in your family is gone during the day, look into doggy daycare for your pup. It's a great way for your Lab to get to know other people and dogs and to learn how to behave away from home.

CHAPTER SIX

Potty Procedures

One of the first things that you have to teach your puppy is when and where to go to the bathroom. Start early and stay consistent in your potty training, and it will help your puppy avoid a lot of confusion (and you a lot of headache) down the road. Your whole family will need to participate in house-training your Labrador Retriever, so the key is for everyone to be patient. With the help of a crate and correct training techniques, your Lab will be potty-trained in no time.

The Great Crate Debate

A dog crate is an important and useful tool to house-train your new puppy. All dogs like to have their own private space that feels comfortable and safe, somewhere to retreat to whenever they want. They will use this space whenever they are feeling sad, worried, or tired.

Your Labrador puppy will try hard not to poop or pee in his crate because dogs naturally want to keep their living and sleeping spaces clean. Because of this, the crate is the perfect house-training tool. Your Lab's crate will also be a safe place to keep your dog when you are not home or when you are traveling with him in your car. It's also a comfortable place for your dog to spend some time alone.

First Thing's First

Show your puppy his crate as soon as he comes home so he learns that it's his new "house." For the first few days, toss a few dog treats into the crate so your puppy will go inside. Pick a crate command to say, such as "Inside" or "Crate," and use this word every time he enters the crate. He will soon remember this word and go inside his crate when you say it. You also can feed him his first few meals inside the crate with the door open so that the puppy will see his crate as a positive, fun place.

Your puppy should sleep in his crate from his very first night. He may cry or whine at first, but don't let him out! If you do, your Labrador Retriever will think that when he makes noise and howls, he will be rewarded by getting out of his crate. It's best to put the crate next to your bed for the first few weeks. Knowing that you're near will make your puppy feel more comfortable and safe. You'll also wake up when your puppy needs to make a midnight potty trip. Whatever you do, don't let your puppy into bed with you at night. You need to show your puppy that you are the leader, and letting your Lab sleep in your bed will make it harder to train him in the long run.

Let your puppy know that you're happy with his potty-training progress with lots of praise and positive reinforcement whenever he correctly goes to the bathroom outside.

A PIECE OF HISTORY

The Labrador Retriever was first recognized by the American Kennel Club in 1917. The Kennel Club of Britain recognized the breed in 1903.

Pups twelve weeks and younger must go to the bathroom at least ten times a day. They require extra attention and planning from you in their early life.

Always put your puppy into his crate for naps, at nighttime, and whenever you are not around to watch him closely. Don't worry; he will let you know when he needs to go outside for a potty trip. If he falls asleep under the table and wakes up when you're not there, guess what he'll do first? By using the crate, you can control when and where your puppy goes to the bathroom.

Repeat, Repeat, Repeat!

By watching your puppy closely and repeating the same commands over and over, your puppy will soon learn that he needs to do his business outside. Puppies younger than twelve weeks old need to go to the bathroom a lot, almost ten times a day! They always need to go potty as soon as they wake up, within a few minutes after eating, after playing with you for a short time, and after being alone in a room or crate.

Always take your Labrador outside to the same area in your yard whenever he needs to go to the bathroom, telling him "Outside" as you go out. This should be a different area from where he plays, if possible. Pick a potty phrase, such as "Go potty" or "Get busy," and use it whenever he does his business. Be sure to get excited, clap your hands, and say "Good puppy!" every time your Lab goes to the

Water Tip

Pick up your puppy's water dish after 7 p.m. This will help your puppy from having to go to the bathroom so much at night. If he gets thirsty, offer him an ice cube. Most Labradors love ice, and your puppy will soon come running every time he hears the ice machine rattle in the kitchen.

Crazy About Crates

bathroom in the correct spot. Use the same door to the backyard every time your puppy needs to go outside so that he will start to remember the way.

Watch for signs that your Lab needs to go pee or poop—sniffing the carpet or circling the floor. Don't let him roam around the house until he's fully house-trained; he won't be able to find that outside door fast enough if he's on the opposite side of the house and the need to poop or pee hits him. He doesn't know your house well enough yet.

Accidents Happen

Your puppy will have accidents. A lot of accidents. All puppies do. When you catch your puppy relieving himself in the house, clap your hands loudly and say "Aaah! Aaah!" Your loud voice should startle him and make him stop until you can pick him up and quickly take him outside. Be sure to get excited and pet your pup when he finishes going to the bathroom outside in the right spot.

If your puppy has an accident in the house and you missed catching him in the act, it's too late. Don't get mad or yell at your Labrador. If you don't catch him while he is going to the bathroom, he won't understand why he is in trouble. Getting mad at him will only confuse and scare him. Just clean up the spot and try to watch your puppy more closely next time.

Never rub your puppy's nose in the accident or hit him when he goes to the bathroom in the house. Your puppy won't understand why he is being punished,

Puppies need to relieve themselves after every playtime, every nap, and every feeding session.

No Crate? No Problem!

If your family doesn't want to use a crate, what can you do with your puppy when you're not home? Use baby gates to close off an area of your house, and place your puppy in this area when you need to leave him alone. Puppy-proof the area by removing anything he can chew on or hurt himself with. Even in a puppy-proofed area, some Lab pups will chew through walls or drywall if they are bored.

You can also buy a small exercise pen from a local pet store that is about 4x4-feet square. This sturdy pen will provide a safe area where you can leave your dog for a short time if you need to. Remember to place some newspapers or pee pads in the area for your dog if he needs to go to the bathroom; also, include a blanket and some safe chew toys to keep him comfortable and happy while you're gone.

Teach your dog to potty in a specific location outdoors, and you will have many happy, accident-free years together.

and he will become scared or angry. Your Lab only wants to please you, and he will learn to stay away from you if you are mean or hurtful. Be nice to your puppy! Remember that he is still learning.

Clean It Up!

Cleaning pet waste accidents in the home is a bit of an art form. There's a technique to removing stains and odors so that, when done properly, your carpet can look and smell as good as new.

When dealing with urine, you must sop up as much of the liquid as possible. Keep old rags or designated towels on hand for this job. Then, saturate the area in whatever cleanser you prefer. Enzyme-based cleaning products work best to break down the chemicals in the waste. If you don't, your Labrador will catch the scent and be drawn to mark the area again and again. Cleaning with white vinegar can get this done, too. Just be sure to avoid ammonia-based cleansers because ammonia is a component in urine and using such a cleaner will simply exacerbate the elimination problem.

After you've applied the cleanser, use a clean towel to blot the area again. Then, grab yet another dry towel to leave on the spot overnight with something heavy stacked on top of it to press the towel into the carpet and draw up any additional moisture. When the soiled area is completely dry, sprinkle it with baking soda and vacuum the area to capture any remaining moisture. It's a long process, to be sure, but cleaning the mess right is well worth it.

If your puppy's accident is more of the solid variety, use a towel or rag to pick up as much of the mess as possible. Dump the stool in the toilet (rather than the ever-tempting trash can), and wash the towel in hot water when you get a chance. Once you've removed as much of the waste as possible, apply the cleanser of your choice and use another towel to soak up any remaining waste particles. Follow the same instructions for cleaning the urine stain from this point on to ensure the area is fully dry. Until your Labrador puppy is completely house-trained, it's a good idea to have your carpet regularly cleaned by a professional.

Paper Training

Most pet trainers agree that teaching a puppy to use a puppy pad or paper for indoor elimination and then retraining him to potty outside can be extremely confusing for the dog. Some dogs never fully grasp the concept that they are supposed to stop using the paper and start using the

No More Mess!

Use these quick tips to keep your house clean while house-training your puppy.

• If you don't have any professional cleaners on hand, create your own using ¼ cup of white vinegar to 1 quart of water.

• Salt will absorb fresh urine and remove some of the scent.

• In a pinch, rubbing the area with a dryer sheet can remove some of the odor.

• White toothpaste can sometimes remove some tough stains from carpet. But beware: it can also ruin the fabric's coloring! It's best never to use toothpaste on dark-colored carpets.

Ring My Bell

Part of housetraining is being able to read your puppy's potty cues before he has an accident. All dogs have different ways of telling you they need to go. Some bark or run to the door, while others more subtly twitch or stare off into space.

If you want to skip these signals altogether, you can try teaching your Labrador to ring a bell when he wants to go outside. To teach this trick, hang a bell on the doorknob or the wall next to the door that you always use to go to your dog's potty area. Make sure the bell is within your puppy's reach. Every time you take him on a potty run, ring the bell before you walk out the door. Eventually, your pup will make the connection and start ringing the bell on his own. When he does, praise him and take him outside. The positive reinforcement will stick, and soon your Lab's potty cues will be clear as a bell.

grass, and they end up mistakenly turning any pile of paper they see into a toilet. However, sometimes paper-training is inevitable, especially if you live in a high-rise building or are unable to regularly walk your dog.

If paper training is the answer for you, spread a few layers of paper (or lay out a puppy training pad) in the area you want your puppy to go. Then place him on this spot when he looks like he needs to go and give him lots of praise when he's done. If you're having trouble training your pup to return to the correct spot, try capturing some of his urine with a sponge and wiping it on the papers to attract him to the scent. There are also some pee pads available that are designed to help induce elimination. When the pad is placed on the papers, its scent is supposed to encourage the puppy to urinate there.

Crate Limits

The crate is a great teaching tool, but make sure to limit how long you put your Lab in it. Labrador Retriever puppies younger than twelve weeks old should never be put in their crate for more than two hours at a time (unless, of course, they are sleeping!). A good rule to follow is three hours maximum for a three-month-old pup, four to five hours for the four- or five-month-old pup, and no more than six hours for Labs over six months of age. If no one in your household can come home to let your Lab out during the day, ask a neighbor or a relative to stop by and let the dog out to go to the bathroom and to get some exercise.

Most importantly, never use the crate for punishment. In order to use a crate for house-training, your puppy must like his crate and see it as his own personal "house." If your puppy sees his crate as a place that he is forced to go when he is bad, he won't want to use it at all. He definitely won't see it as a safe place where he can go when he is tired, worried, or afraid.

Sure, you can put your puppy in his crate after he has made a mess in the house while you clean up. Just don't be angry or say "bad dog" when you put him inside. Always let your dog know that the crate is a happy place of comfort and fun.

House-training is best taught by repeating the same actions and commands and by watching your puppy closely. The more times you show your puppy where to go potty, the more he will remember to go in the right place. Most of all, your Lab puppy wants to make you happy; so be patient and let your puppy know that even though he may make mistakes, he is still your favorite furry pal!

Consistency is key to all successful puppy training endeavors. Take your pup to the same potty spot every time until he eventually learns to go there himself.

At a Glance ...

The crate is a great tool to use for house-training your Labrador Retriever when it is used correctly and humanely.

· ·

Be sure that you never use the crate to punish your dog. Your Lab should see his crate as a happy place where he can go to feel safe and comfortable.

· ·

Take your puppy outside often to go potty. Remember that puppies under twelve weeks old need to go to the bathroom every two hours.

· ·

Young puppies can't "hold it" for long, so watch for your Labrador Retriever's signals that he needs to go out. If he has an accident, don't get mad; just clean it up and promise to watch him more closely next time.

· ·

Get excited when your puppy goes potty outside! Your Labrador wants to make you happy, and if you show him that going to the bathroom in the yard makes you happy, he will want to do it all the time!

CHAPTER SEVEN

Basic Training Boot Camp

If you want everyone to love your Labrador Retriever and be pleased to see him, you need to teach him good doggy manners. Manners for a Lab mean coming, sitting, staying, lying down, and heeling (walking at your side) when you ask him to—always.

As soon as your Lab puppy comes home, start teaching him the *come, sit, stay, lie down,* and *heel* cues. Don't worry, he's not too young. In fact, puppyhood is the best time to begin

teaching him! Puppies are like sponges; they are ready to absorb all that you can teach them. The earlier you start, the easier it will be.

The Secret Weapon

Before you can really teach your Lab any cue, two things must happen: your puppy must learn his name (name recognition) and you must be able to get and hold his attention. To do this, you must have a secret weapon: treats (aka, tiny tasty tidbits of something soft and easy to chew)! But you must be careful not to overfeed your Labrador, or he'll become a pudgy pup. Thin slices of hot dogs cut into four pieces work well, as does plain popcorn (no butter or salt). Even raw veggies, like baby carrots, tempt the taste buds of some dogs (and in a healthy way!).

To begin, call your Lab puppy's name once: "Jake." Do not repeat it two or three times: "Jake-Jake-Jake." Just say it once. Otherwise, he will learn that he has a three-part name and will ignore you when you say the name once. You should use his name when he is not distracted by other things. That way, he will be sure to react by looking at you; when he does, quickly flip him a treat. Repeat about a dozen times, several times a day. It won't take more than a day or two before he understands that his name equals something good to eat.

Throughout the training process, reward your dog with small treats and other positive reinforcement.

Training Tip No. 1: Quiet, Please

Always start your teaching exercises in a quiet place. No TV, no music, no other animals. Think about when you learn or study. Don't you learn more when there's nothing else going on around you? Once your Labrador pup has learned a cue, such as *come*, take him to a different room and practice the cue there. When he is obeying you in that room, ask another person to hang around or bring another animal into the room while you try the cue. If your puppy reacts to the other person or animal and does not obey your cue, go back to teaching the cue in a quiet room for a while. When you think your puppy is ready for you to try again, ask your friend or family member to come back.

Training Tip No. 2: One on One

Only one person should train the puppy at first. If more than one person is telling your Labrador Retriever what to do, he might get confused. Remember, dogs like to know who the leader of the pack is. Too many leaders can mean that your dog will end up just scratching his head (with his paw, no doubt!) not knowing what to do. Once your puppy has really learned a cue, however, other family members can and should join in the training sessions.

Ignore Your Lab

Before you begin a training lesson, pretend to ignore your Lab puppy for a few minutes. This will make your dog want your attention even more. By the time you do give your pup attention for a quick training session, he will be really eager for your company and willing to listen to what you say. Perfect!

Did You Know?

A Labrador Retriever's color has nothing to do with his temperament. All Labradors are kind, outgoing, and eager to please—regardless of whether they are yellow, chocolate, or black.

Training Tip No. 3: Keep It Short

Be sure to keep lessons short so your puppy won't get bored. Again, think about how bored you get if a lesson goes on and on. In time, your Lab (like you) will be able to concentrate for longer periods. Watch for signs of boredom and loss of attention—if your Lab is looking around at other things, that's when you know it's time to stop. Do the exercises in slightly different ways to keep him eager to learn. Remember, you don't like to do the exact same things over and over, either!

Training Tip No. 4: Always Praise

Always keep your puppy's lessons upbeat. Use praise, lots of praise, and even more praise! Never train your puppy or adult dog when you are grumpy. If you're in a bad mood, you may lose your temper when your puppy doesn't do what

Once you have mastered the basic commands, you can practice your sessions off lead and in a location with many potential distractions.

you want him to and you might scold him or yell at him. Thinking you are mad at him, he may tuck his tail and cower. Any progress the two of you have made during training will be lost, and your pup will start disliking his lessons instead of enjoying the time with you.

Training Tip No. 5: End Positively

Finally, finish every training session on a positive note. If you have been struggling or unsuccessful, switch gears and do something he knows well (like *sit!*) to end the session.

Now, On to the Cues

Before you begin teaching the cues, pick a release word to tell your dog that the lesson is over for the day, something like "At ease!" as they say in the military.

"All done," "Free," and "OK" are the words most commonly used for dogs. You'll need this release word or phrase so your Lab will know that the lesson is finished and it's fine to relax. Once you have the release word or phrase picked, you can start teaching your Lab the basic cues.

Take It and Leave It

Begin by placing a treat in the palm of your hand and saying "Take it" as your pup grabs the treat. Repeat three times. On the fourth time, do not say a word as your Labrador reaches for the treat; just close your fingers around the treat and wait. Do not pull away, but be ready for the pup to paw, lick, bark, and nibble your fingers. Be patient! When he finally pulls away from your hand and waits for a few seconds, open your hand and tell him to "Take it." Repeat the hand-closing exercise until he waits for you to say "Take it."

Now, show your Lab the treat in the palm of your hand and tell him to "Leave it." When he goes for the treat, close your hand and repeat "Leave it." Repeat this step until he pulls away, then wait just a second, open your hand, tell him to "Take it," and allow him to grab the treat. Repeat saying "Leave it" until he waits just a few seconds, then give him the treat on "Take it." Gradually extend the time that you wait after your puppy leaves it and before you tell him to "Take it."

If you decide to reward with food treats, pick something small, only giving your dog a taste of it so that he will want to continue training to get more treats.

While practicing the various training cues, keep your Labrador Retriever on the leash. It will help you redirect any misbehavior.

Now you want to teach your Labrador to leave things on the ground, not just in your hand. Think of all the things you don't want him to pick up. Put your puppy on a leash and hold it loosely. Now stand in front of him and toss a treat behind you and a little to the side, so he can see it while you say "Leave it." If he goes for the treat, block him with your body, not your hands; stepping forward to move him back away from the treat. As soon as he backs off and gives up trying to get around you, unblock the treat and tell him to "Take it." Be ready to block again if he goes for it before you give permission. Repeat the process until he understands and waits for the cue.

The *leave it* cue also teaches your dog to ignore an item that he comes across and takes an interest in. Here's another technique to teach the cue: With your Lab on a leash, walk by a tempting item (such as food or toys that you've set up to encounter along the way). When your dog tries to pick it up, give a short, quick tug on his leash and say "Leave it!" Reward and praise him once he obeys. Repeat and reinforce the command often.

Once your Lab leaves treats until you tell him to take them, teach him the same cue with his food dish. With the dish on the floor behind you, tell your pup to "Leave it." Once he does this right, tell him to "Take it" (he can either sit or stand while waiting for his dish).

As before, make him wait a little longer each time before you tell him to "Take it."

This reminds your Lab that you're the leader and that all good things, like food, come from you, the person who loves him. The lesson with the food bowl will help keep your puppy from becoming possessive of his food bowl—growling if you try to take it from him or come too close to it—a behavior that only worsens over time and can lead to very bad behavior. A dog should never growl at his owner! The safety and good-behavior benefits of a solid *Take it*/*Leave it* are endless.

Drop It

Similarly, when your Lab picks up something that he shouldn't touch, tell him to "Drop it!" and walk over to him. Don't run, or he'll think you're starting a game of chase. If your dog refuses to drop it, physically open his mouth yourself and remove the item. Once your Lab does let go of the item, praise him and give him a safe alternative item as a substitute, such as a favorite toy or treat. Repetition and positive reinforcement are key to this technique, as well.

Dogs try to eat the most ridiculous things sometimes; rat poison, rotten food, household gardening solutions—believe it or not, it all looks appealing to your dog. And while your Labrador might discover (after indulging his craving, of course) that he doesn't actually have an appetite for your car's fuel injection cleaner, the toxic damage will have already been done. The *leave it* and *drop it* cues could very well help save your dog's life some day.

Come Cue

This is another cue that could save your Labrador Retriever's life. If, for instance, your dog suddenly takes off after a squirrel he just *has* to chase and runs into the street, you need to get him to come back to you instantly. No playing in the street for him! Or what if a skunk wanders into your backyard and your dog starts to go after him? Unless you want a very stinky dog to bathe (which takes a lot of hard work—skunk spray is disgusting and stays around for a long time!), you'd better have a dog that will stop right away and come to you.

Always practice the *come* cue on leash and in a safely confined area, like a fenced backyard. You can't risk failure, or the pup will learn that he does not have to come when called. That could be a disaster—remember that skunk! Use a long leash for teaching this cue.

Keep hold of the leash, walk a short distance away from your Lab, then get his attention by calling his name or making a noise. Once the pup is focused on

Be Safe and Be Happy

The *leave it* cue is important for letting a dog know who is the leader, as well as for his safety. Dogs, especially puppies, like to explore the world with their mouths. But that can be very dangerous.

If you are walking your dog and you come across a dead bird or a discarded piece of food, the last thing you want is for your Lab to put it in his mouth! That could make him very sick. You want to quickly say "Leave it" and know your dog will respond. A Lab that will leave it on cue is a Lab likely to live a healthy life (and have a better taste in his mouth!).

Once your Labrador Retriever has learned the *sit* cue, experiment with the amount of time he stays sitting to teach him patience before receiving his reward.

you, call him: "Puppy, come!" (use your happy voice) and give him a treat when he comes to you. If he hesitates or doesn't come, tug him to you gently with his leash. Grasp and hold his collar with one hand, as you give him the treat with the other. The collar grasp is important. This maneuver also connects holding his collar with coming and treating, which will assist you in countless future behaviors. After using treats several times, you will phase out the treat and switch to hands-on praise (offering your puppy a pat or a stroke) only.

Do ten or twelve repetitions, two or three times a day. Once your pup has mastered the *come* cue, continue to practice every day to be sure this cue sticks in his young puppy brain!

Sit Cue

This cue is easy because your Lab already understands that obeying you means he gets a treat. To begin, stand in front of your pup, move the treat right over his nose, and then slowly move it backward over his head. As your dog's head moves back to reach the goody, his rear will move toward the ground. If your Lab raises up to reach the treat, simply lower it a bit to keep it within sitting distance. The second his rump touches the floor, tell him "Sit." Then, release the treat and gently grasp his collar, as you did with the *come* cue. Your dog will again make that positive connection between the treat, the sit position, and the collar hold. Practice until your dog gives you the correct response quickly and effortlessly.

The *stay* cue has many practical applications, such as keeping your dog on the curb until it's safe to cross a busy street.

Can Your Dog Pass the Canine Good Citizen® Test?

Once your Lab is ready for advanced training, you can start training him for the American Kennel Club Canine Good Citizen® program. This program is for dogs that are trained to behave at home, out in the neighborhood, and in the city. It's easy and fun to do. Once your dog learns basic obedience and good canine manners, a CGC evaluator gives your dog ten basic tests. If he passes, he's awarded a Canine Good Citizen® certificate. Many trainers offer classes with the test as the final "graduation" class. To find an evaluator in your area, go to www.akc.org/events/cgc/cgc_bystate.cfm.

Many therapy dogs and guide dogs are required to pass the Canine Good Citizen® test in order to help as working dogs in the community. There are ten specific tests that a dog must pass in order to pass the Canine Good Citizen® test. A well-trained dog will:

1. Let a friendly stranger approach and talk to his owner.
2. Let a friendly stranger pet him.
3. Be comfortable being groomed and examined by a friendly stranger.
4. Walk on a leash and show that he is in control and not overly excited.
5. Move through a crowd politely and confidently.
6. Sit and stay on command.
7. Come when called.
8. Behave calmly around another dog.
9. Not bark at or react to a surprise distraction.
10. Show that he can be left with a trusted person away from his owner.

In order to help your dog pass the AKC CGC test, first enroll him in a series of basic training classes and CGC training classes. You can find classes and trainers near you by searching the AKC website. When you feel that your Lab is ready to take the test, locate an AKC-approved CGC evaluator to set up a test date, or sign up for a test that is held at a local AKC dog show or training class. For more information about the AKC Canine Good Citizen® program, visit the website at www.akc.org/events.cgc.

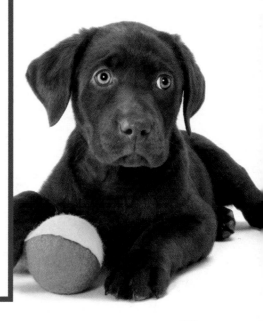

The *down* cue can be a tough one to master, because it requires your Lab's submission. But it helps to calm an easily excitable dog when necessary.

As your Lab becomes better at sitting, make him hold the sit position for longer periods of time before you give him the treat. (Holding the sit position is the first part of the *stay* cue.) Begin using your release word or phrase—"OK," "All done," or "Free"—to release him from the sit position. Practice using the *sit* cue daily for things such as sitting for his food bowl or a toy, and have your dog practice sits throughout the day, always for a food or praise reward. Once you can count on him to obey, combine saying "Sit" and "Leave it" for his food dish.

Stay Cue

If your Labrador Retriever knows how to sit, it's easy to get him to stay—the dog's understanding for needing to *stay* comes from the same behavioral modification for *sit*. With your puppy sitting when cued, place the palm of your hand in front of his nose and tell him to "Stay." Count to five. Give him his release word to end the stay and praise him. Stretch out the stays bit by bit. Puppies have a lot of energy, however, so he may only be able to stay for a short time at first. Be patient!

Once you can count on your Lab to stay while you stand in front of him, tell him to "Stay," then take a step backward, then a step forward again. You want him to stay while you move. If your Lab pup moves, say "No" and stand in front of him. Try again, until he stays when you move. Slowly, you can step farther away from your puppy while having him stay.

Down Cue

The *down* cue can be a tough one. Some Labs and other take-charge breeds may find it really difficult to do because it is a "submissive posture," meaning the dog is really admitting that you are his leader! That's why it's very important to teach the *down* cue when your Lab is very young.

With your puppy in the sit position, move the food lure from his nose to the ground and slightly backward between his front paws. Wiggle it to spark his interest. As soon as his front legs and rear end hit the floor, give him the treat and tell him "Down, good boy, down!" Remember, *down* may be difficult for your dog, so be patient and give him lots and lots praise when he does what you want. Once he goes into the down position with no problem, use the *stay* cue with it. By six months of age, your puppy should be able to do a ten-minute solid *sit/stay;* and a ten-minute *down/stay.*

Wait Cue

Have you ever had to clean up after your Labrador Retriever when he trots into the house with wet or muddy paws? If you have, then you will really love the *wait* cue! It should freeze your dog in his muddy tracks!

Begin working on the *wait* cue with a door inside the house, one that leads from one room to another. With your Lab behind you, start to open the door as if you are going to go through it. When your dog tries to follow, step in front of him, using your body to block him from going through. Don't use the word "wait" just yet. Keep blocking until he hesitates and you can open the door a little to slip through. Then say your wait release word, "Through" or "OK" or whatever release word you have chosen for this exercise, and let him go through the door. Repeat by body-blocking until he understands and waits for you, then start saying "Wait" when he stops and waits for you. Practice in different doorways; then try it with an outside entrance. Have him wait outside the back door (if you have a fenced yard).

Heel Cue

A young Labrador Retriever should be taught to walk politely on a leash, at or near your side. That is best taught when your pup is very young and small, before he can pull you down the street! (Which may look pretty funny when it's happening to someone else, but is not a position you want to be in!) The formal *heel* cue will come later.

Start leash training soon after your puppy comes home. Let him get used to the leash by clipping it to his buckle collar and letting him drag it around for a little while every day. Make wearing his leash a happy moment in your Lab's day by playing a game with him while it's on. If he chews the leash, distract him with a play activity. You also can stop chewing by spraying the leash with a bitter product to make it taste unpleasant (these products can be found at your local pet-supply store.)

After a few days, attach the leash and take your Lab to a place in your house or yard where the two of you can be alone. Now, pick up the leash. With your puppy on your left side, hold a treat lure at his eye level to get him to walk next

Graduating with Honors

The Labrador Retriever is an amazing breed that can be taught to do great things once he's learned basic good behavior (the cues in this chapter). He can be trained to be an assistance dog, who helps people with physical challenges, like those who can't walk and are in wheelchairs or who have lost their eyesight or hearing. For people in wheelchairs, trained Labs can retrieve dropped items or get things off counters that the people can't reach. Guide dogs help their blind owners go around obstacles, safely cross streets, and even find things, such as doors. Hearing dogs can alert their deaf owners to ringing doorbells and other important sounds.

A Warning

Experienced Labrador Retriever owners know that they can never completely trust their dog to come when called if he is off leash and intently focused on a mission of his own (like chasing a squirrel). The term "off-leash" often means out of control. Always keep your Labrador Retriever on a leash when he is not in a fenced or confined area. If he does manage to escape from you elsewhere, use the *come* cue firmly and quickly.

to you. Pat your knee and use a happy voice. Say "Let's go!" as you move forward, holding the treat low to keep him near. Take a few steps, give the treat, and tell your Lab what a good dog he is! Move forward just a few steps each time.

Keep these sessions short and happy, no more than thirty seconds at a time (that's long in puppy time). Never scold him into walking faster or slower, just cheer him on with happy talk. Walk straight ahead at first, adding wide turns once he gets the hang of walking at your side. Progress to sharp right or left turns, using a gentle leash tug on the turns, a happy verbal "Let's go!" and, of course, a treat. Walk in short ten- to twenty-second bursts with a break (use your release word) and brief play (hugs will suffice) in between. Keep total training time short and always quit with success, even if after just a few short steps.

School Is Cool

All of these behaviors are taught in some phase of a young-dog training class. Check with your veterinarian, pet store, or a local kennel club to find a puppy kindergarten or basic obedience class in your area. Clubs may also hold special training seminars.

Keep a few things in mind: Learn all you can. There are dozens of books written on positive training methods. You and your Labrador will both be smarter

Obedience classes can be a big help in teaching you proper training techniques and in reinforcing good behavior expectations.

for your efforts. Ongoing practice is actually a lifetime canine rule, especially for a strong-willed Lab. Dogs will be dogs, and if we don't make sure that they keep up their skills, they will slip back into sloppy behaviors, not paying attention, and will be more difficult to correct. Make these cues part of your daily routine, and your Labrador Retriever will remain a polite companion that you can be proud of.

Beyond the Basics

Once you've experienced the fun of socializing your young puppy and started basic training exercises like *sit* and *stay* you may ask yourself, "What's next?"

The best way to answer that question is to find an American Kennel Club dog club in your area. Many of these clubs offer basic obedience classes, puppy kindergarten, or even the AKC S.T.A.R. Puppy Program. These programs will help give your Lab a great foundation to becoming a valued family companion. To find a class or instructor, search the AKC website's training clubs online directory at www.akc.org/events/obedience/training_clubs. You can search by state for clubs or training classes near you. Tell the club representative that you'd like to get your puppy off on the right paw for training! They'll be happy to help you. You can also search for a trainer that teaches the AKC Canine Good Citizen Program. This program encourages responsible pet ownership and rewards dogs with good manners.

Agility and other fun canine sporting events await you and your Labrador Retriever once he has mastered basic behavior training.

Training your dog helps to deepen the canine-human bond, and further training becomes even more fulfilling for both owner and Labrador (who thrives from doing jobs to help others). In order to train and learn new things with your dog, you must strengthen your communication skills.

The best way to use the skills that you and your Labrador have mastered after completing the Canine Good Citizen test might be to try a fun, new activity like AKC Rally, the Beginner Novice Obedience Class, or America's fastest growing dog sport—Agility! An AKC dog club can help you find classes for these activities, too. There, you can also find other dog owners who enjoy doing the same things you like, such as traveling with your dog to classes or shows, as well as meeting new dogs and their owners.

Once you have a happy, well-trained Labrador Retriever, what should you do next? Show him off to the world, of course! And there is no better place for that than at an AKC event. (See chapter 11 for a rundown of great activities for your Labrador Retriever and you.)

Does your angelic dog follow your every beck and call? Why not train him to be an AKC Canine Good Citizen and make it official.

At a Glance ...

A solid foundation in the basic cues is the first step to transform your Labrador Retriever into a well-mannered canine good citizen.

. . . .

Before beginning any lesson, your pup must recognize his name, and you must be able to get and keep his attention.

. . . .

Training "Take it" and "Leave it" helps you control what goes into your Lab's mouth—and Labs love to put things in their mouths!

. . . .

The basic cues include *come, sit, stay, down, heel*, and *wait*.

. . . .

Make practice part of your daily routine to keep your Lab sharp and reliable. You will find many opportunities each day to reinforce your dog's knowledge of the cues he's learned.

. . . .

What's next for your Lab? Find out more about obedience, agility, rally and dog shows. Your Lab will be glad you looked into all of these exciting AKC events for both of you.

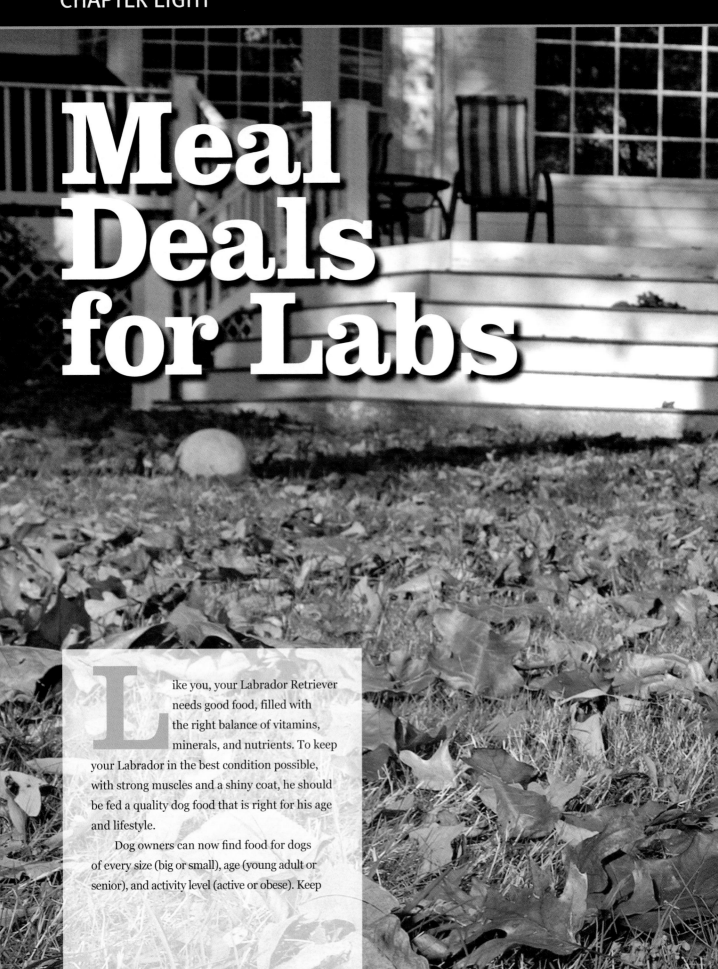

CHAPTER EIGHT

Meal Deals for Labs

Like you, your Labrador Retriever needs good food, filled with the right balance of vitamins, minerals, and nutrients. To keep your Labrador in the best condition possible, with strong muscles and a shiny coat, he should be fed a quality dog food that is right for his age and lifestyle.

Dog owners can now find food for dogs of every size (big or small), age (young adult or senior), and activity level (active or obese). Keep

in mind that puppies need a different diet than adults dogs. After all, you wouldn't feed a steak dinner to a baby, so why would you feed an adult dog's dinner to a puppy?

When shopping for the best dog food, new owners should look for puppy growth formulas with appropriate amounts of protein and fat for the different breed sizes. Large, fast-growing dogs like Labrador Retrievers require less protein and fat during their early puppy months (less protein and fat are better for healthy joints). Medium and small breeds likewise have different nutritional requirements during their first year of growth than they do as adults.

The Right Food

Dog owners shouldn't be scared by all the different dog foods on the store shelves, worrying that they won't be able to pick the right one. Instead, talk to your veterinarian or breeder about which food would be best for your Lab pup.

What exactly is in your dog's food? You can find out by reading the labels. The ingredients will be listed in order of the most important to the least important, which means that the main ingredient is the first one listed and all others are listed in descending order, according to the amount included in the food. If beef is the most important ingredient, for example, it will be listed first on the label, and so forth.

Don't forget the importance of water. All dogs, especially active Labs, should have constant access to fresh water.

If you want even more information, check with your veterinarian or the websites of dog food manufacturers. Owners must learn as much as they can from the experts about what to feed their Labrador Retrievers.

Necessary Nutrients

Dogs' bodies work much like as ours. Here's a breakdown of everything your Labrador Retriever needs in his diet to stay healthy for years to come:

- **Proteins** are used for growth and repair of muscles, bones, and other body tissues. They also help produce antibodies, enzymes, and hormones.
- **Carbohydrates** are metabolized by the body into glucose, which is the body's main energy source.
- **Fats** provide the body with energy when no glucose is available. They are also important for proper function of the nervous system, the production of hormones, and vitamin support.
- **Vitamins** and **minerals** both participate in the body's muscle and nerve functions, as well as assist in bone growth, healing, metabolism, and the balance of fluids.
- And don't forget **water**. All dogs, great and small, require plenty of fresh drinking water to keep their bodies functioning at optimal performance and to

avoid dehydration during extreme heat or exercise. Your Lab should probably be drinking at least one ounce of water per pound of body weight each day, as a good rule of thumb. Hot weather or vigorous exercise can double or sometimes even triple that requirement, though. Give your dog ample access to fresh water throughout the day.

When choosing food for your Lab, keep his age and weight in mind. A puppy has different nutritional requirements than an adult or senior dog.

Complete and Balanced

Your Labrador Retriever will thrive best on a complete and balanced diet, so look for food formulas labeled as such. The Association of American Feed Control Officials has standardized the requirements for appropriate canine food formulas. Only foods that have been approved by the AAFCO are allowed to be labeled as "complete and balanced" diets, meaning that they meet the nutritional standards

A PIECE OF HISTORY

In 1830, noted British sportsman Colonel Hawker described the Lab as "the best for any kind of shooting...very fine in legs, with short, smooth hair...is extremely quick running, swimming, and fighting...and their sense of smell is hardly to be credited."

Limit the People Food!

As a general rule, do not feed your Lab people food, especially spicy, prepared foods. A lot of what we eat is dangerous for a dog to eat. While it's perfectly okay to add cooked carrots, chicken, or brown rice to your dog's dinner bowl, foods such as chocolate, onions, grapes, and nuts will make your Lab very ill.

Examine the label carefully when choosing your Labrador's food. After all, it's the fuel that will get him through his active day!

for dogs at their various stages of life. Manufacturers earn this label either by conducting strictly controlled feeding trials or by matching their products to a well-detailed nutrient profile.

A "complete and balanced" diet consists of the proper proportion of vitamis, minerals, fats, protein, and carbohydrates necessary to promote your dog's growth and good health. Your dog's size and activity level will determine the amount of food he needs each day. Start by giving your Labrador the amount of food that is suggested on the food's label, but keep an eye on your dog while he eats. Sometimes a big, active dog like the Labrador Retriever will need more food than is recommended, but often the portion suggested is larger than necessary.

Changing Dog Foods

When you bring your new Lab home, be careful about changing to a completely different dog food right away. That quick change could make your dog sick. If you plan to switch from the food fed by his breeder, take home a small supply of the breeder's food to mix with your own. Make the change slowly to aid your puppy's adjustment to his new food.

It's important to feed your Lab puppy three times a day to aid his growth and digestion. Feed your adult Lab twice a day, in the morning and at night.

Problems with Free-Feeding

If you leave a bowl of food out for your Labrador all the time (which is called *free-feeding*), you could turn him into a picky eater—a bite here, a nibble there. He could turn his nose up at the food you offer, demanding something else. Dogs that are free-feeders are also more likely to become possessive of their food bowls. If you come near your dog's food bowl, he could begin growling at you, which is a dog's way of saying "Back off!" Dogs should never growl at their owners, as it could lead to other more serious behavioral problems of aggression.

Labs love to eat. Your dog will try to convince you to give him more food than he needs, but remember that free-feeding only leads to obesity.

If you notice your Lab's waistline expanding or he appears as skin and bones, you'll need to adjust the portion accordingly. Talk to your veterinarian for advice if you're unsure.

Labrador Retrievers don't really have any special dietary needs, as is the case in some other breeds that are of a similar size. A good food formula that is well-balanced will not require any supplementation. Generally speaking, if you need to supplement something into your Lab's diet, then you might want to look for another good-quality commercial formula available. The same goes for extra vitamins. Be cautious about adding supplements or vitamins to your dog's diet. Consult your veterinarian before adding vitamins, supplements, or herbs to your dog's regular food.

Wet and Dry

The two main types of dog food are wet and dry varieties. Wet food contains more water and often has a higher fat and protein percentage. Dogs tend to want to eat it up, so an all-wet-food diet can easily result in an obese Lab. The biggest advantages of canned wet foods are extensive variety, taste appeal, and a long shelf life. However, it's typically much more expensive than dry food.

While the variety of dry foods isn't nearly as comprehensive as wet formulas, it has other benefits that canned food lacks. The crunchy texture of dry kibble helps clear the plaque and tartar off dogs' teeth. However, dry food contains preservatives and tends to be high in carbohydrates, often listing soybean, corn or other bulky starches as the main ingredients. Proportionately, dry foods are the most calorie- and nutrient-dense, so you need more of a canned food product to provide the same amount of nutrition.

Many owners choose to add a little water or wet food to their dogs' kibble on occasion to spice up the flavor without changing its texture.

Lifestage Foods

Lifestage formulas have grown in popularity in recent years. You'll find many types marketed on store shelves, such as growth formula (for puppies) and maintenance formula (for adult dogs). Ask your veterinarian's advice before starting your Lab on any specialty food varieties beyond these.

- **Puppy diets:** Growth formulas provide higher levels of fat and protein to sustain a young dog's normal growth rate. According to the AAFCO, the formula must contain at least 22 percent protein.
- **Adult diets:** AAFCO-approved adult maintenance diets must have at least 18 percent protein and 5 percent fat. Performance formulas can sometimes contain up to 30 percent protein, 20 percent fat, and more than 1,500 calories per pound. Talk to your veterinarian before deciding what type of food is right for your dog.
- **Senior diets:** Older, less active dogs need fewer calories. The protein and fat content in these formulas can vary.

How Many Meals?

If you leave it up to your dog, he will have you feeding him every second of the day! Labs, with their big eyes, are really good at making you believe they are starving all the time. Don't let them fool you! If you do, you will end up with a chubby chowhound who lies around all day. So follow the general rules listed below to make sure you're feeding your Labrador the correct portions.

Rule No. 1: If your Lab is less than twelve weeks of age, he should eat three times a day. When the puppy is about twelve weeks of age, feed him twice a day. Most breeders suggest two meals a day for the life of the dog, regardless of breed, rather than one large meal.

Rule No. 2: A Labrador should be fed at the same times each day. Most owners agree that scheduled meals

work out much better than free-feeding (meaning, leaving the bowl out all day). Scheduled meals are also another chance to remind your Labrador Retriever that all good things in life come from his pack leader. With scheduled meals, it's also easier to predict when your Lab puppy has to go outside to potty, which makes it easier to house-train your dog. Feeding your dog regular meals also will help you keep track of of just how much your puppy eats, which you need to know to control his weight. With regular meals, you'll also notice if your Lab's appetite changes; if he's suddenly not interested in eating his morning or evening meal, it could mean that he is ill. If this happens, consult your veterinarian right away and asked whether your dog should come in for a checkup.

How Much to Feed?

Like people, different dogs have different appetites; some will lick their food bowls clean and beg for more, while others pick at their food and leave some of it untouched. It's easy to overfeed a chowhound. Chubby puppies may be cute and cuddly, but the extra weight will stress their growing joints and may lead to the development of hip and elbow disease. Overweight pups also tend to grow into overweight adults who tire easily and will be more susceptible to other health problems. Breeders and veterinarians can offer advice about how to adjust meal portions as your puppy grows.

An important rule to keep in mind: lean is healthy, fat is not. Research has proven that obesity is a major canine killer. Quite simply, a lean dog lives longer than one who is overweight. And that doesn't even reflect the better quality of life for the lean dog that can run, jump, and play without the burden of an extra ten or twenty pounds.

If your adult dog is overweight, he should be switched to a "light" food, which has fewer calories and more fiber. "Senior" foods for older dogs are made for less active older dogs. "Performance" diets contain more fat and protein for dogs that compete in sports or are very active.

The Dangers of Bloat

Owners of Labradors and other deep-chested breeds need to watch for bloat. This ailment causes a dog's stomach to twist on itself, keeping gas inside and cutting off blood flow. It can lead to shock and death if not treated quickly. Some veterinarians believe that dogs who gulp large amounts of food or drink lots of water right after eating can be in danger of getting bloat. Luckily, it's completely treatable. Make your Lab slow down while he eats. Other bloat-prevention measures include no heavy exercise for at least an hour before eating and two hours afterward. Make sure your dog is not overly excited during meals; nervous and overly excited dogs may be more likely to get this life-threatening condition. A Labrador who tries to vomit but cannot, a dog who is drooling a lot, or a dog that simply looks like he is uncomfortable may be suffering from bloat. Consult your dog's vet about other signs of bloat and ways to keep him from getting it. If you think your Lab may have bloat, he should go to the vet right away.

The Bottom Line

What and how much you choose to feed your Labrador Retriever are major factors in his overall health and how long he lives. His well-being is in your hands. Research the nutritional content of anything you plan to buy, and look beyond the fancy packaging to the labels on the back. Keep treats to a minimum, and be sure to feed your dog the best diet you can. And always consult your veterinarian if you have any questions about your Lab's nutrition.

A lean Lab is a healthy Lab. Keep your dog healthy with the right diet and plenty of exercise. He'll thank you for it with years of companionship.

At a Glance ...

Your Labrador Retriever needs a balanced and complete diet made for large-breed dogs. He will start off on a good puppy formula, then switch to adult food and possibly change to a senior diet as he gets older.

. . . .

Your dog's vet and his breeder are great sources of advice. Discuss with them the correct amount of food to feed your Lab to keep him in good and lean condition. Chubbiness can be dangerous to a dog's health and can shorten his lifespan.

. . . .

Stick to a daily feeding schedule of two meals per day; free-feeding (leaving food out all the time) is not recommended.

. . . .

The deep-chested Labrador is a breed that may be at risk to get bloat. Your vet can tell you how to keep your dog from getting bloat and what signs to watch for.

. . . .

Your Lab's health, coat quality, level of friskiness, and overall condition depend on his diet.

CHAPTER NINE

Grooming Guidelines

Scruffy people and dogs that have unkempt hair, dirty teeth, long nails, and bad breath don't make a lot of friends! Good grooming is not just a matter of looking good and having friends, it's a matter of health. To live a healthy and long life, any Labrador Retriever must be well taken care of.

Brushing your dog's coat and teeth should be a weekly process, and you should check your Lab's ears often for signs of problems. And trim

Good Teeth = Good Health

Home dental care is vital to your Lab's health. Studies prove that good oral hygiene (taking care of your dog's teeth by regular brushing and a check up by the vet) can add three to five years to a dog's life. In other words, brushing means you'll have your Lab around for a lot longer!

his nails monthly. Part of taking care of your dog means understanding how to properly groom him.

It's best to introduce your Labrador to the brush, nail clippers, and toothbrush when he's a pup. Dogs that have not had their coat brushed, nails clipped, ears checked, and teeth cleaned early in life may object when they are older, bigger, and better able to put up a fight!

Start with short amounts of time, stroking your pup gently with a soft brush, briefly handling his paws, looking inside his ears, and gently touching his gums. Use lots of sweet talk and offer little tasty treats to ensure the experience is a positive one for your pup.

Lab, Meet Bath

The adult Labrador Retriever has a short and straight double coat, with an undercoat that varies in thickness depending on the climate in which he lives. He will have a thicker coat in cold weather; a thinner one in warm weather. Brushing once a week will remove dust and spread the oils that keep your Lab's coat clean and healthy. During shedding season (usually springtime), however, you will need to brush your dog's coat more frequently. Consider even brushing him daily, as it will greatly help reduce matting.

The good news is that Labs don't need to be bathed very often; in fact, washing your dog too much will remove essential oils from his skin and coat. Brushing is the best way to remove dust and spread those oils to keep his coat super sheen. You only need to bathe your Labrador Retriever every month or two. Of course, there are other times when you will have to wash your dog, like when he plays in mud or rolls in something stinky!

To make bath time less stressful for your Labrador Retriever when he's an adult—and to keep him from fighting to get away—introduce him to bathing when he's a pup. Luckily, because the breed loves the water, your Labrador Retriever should take to the experience easily.

Labs love water and dirt, which often adds up to one muddy dog. Bath time!

Ease your pup through this acclimation process; don't just stick him in the tub and lather up. Begin by lining the tub or shower with a towel or mat for safe footing. Don't add any water right now; you don't want your puppy to scamper away! Now lure him into the tub with treats. Once your little Labrador learns to be comfortable in the dry tub (give him a day or two), gradually add shallow water, then finally work up to the whole bathing process.

To wash your Labrador, first wet his coat thoroughly, starting at the hindquarters. Use warm water; too hot or too cold will be unpleasant. When you shampoo, use a soap-free one that is made just for dogs that you can find at the pet store. Ask your veterinarian what you should use if you're not sure. Don't use shampoo for people.

Work the shampoo into a good lather all the way down his body. Be sure to scrub through the fur all the way down to his skin, it'll help get rid of dead skin cells and reduce any skin irritation. Use this bath time as an opportunity to check your dog's skin for any bites, bumps, infections, or other abnormalities. Wash his head last, being careful not to get soap and water in his eyes or ear canals.

After shampooing, rinse your dog's coat completely to avoid any itching from leftover residue. Use a towel to dry him off. A chamois (a special kind of towel people use most often to dry cars) works well because it absorbs water like a sponge. You can also use a pet dryer or your own hair dryer to speed up the drying process (make sure to set your dryer on low heat and hold it away from your

Did You Know?

Labs have a water- and weather-resistant coat that tends to be somewhat oily. The oil protects the dog's skin and keeps the coat from becoming waterlogged. That's why, after a dip or bath, a Lab is virtually dry after a few quick shakes.

A roll in the dirt sounds like good fun to the Labrador Retriever, but be sure to check for ticks and other hitchhiking pests before brushing your dog thoroughly and giving him a bath if necessary.

dog). Keep your Lab away from drafts for a while after bathing and drying so that he doesn't get cold.

Minty-Fresh Breath

Brushing teeth is important for dogs. Plaque and tartar buildup can lead to gum disease, which can be the start of more serious diseases of the internal organs, such as the heart. Try brushing your Labrador's pearly whites at least once a week—twice is even better!

As with bathing, you should introduce tooth brushing while your Labrador Retriever is still a puppy. Start by rubbing your finger around his gums and over his puppy teeth. Make it a good experience for him by praising him and petting him often throughout the process.

When your Lab seems ready and used to the sensation, you can start the real brushing, using a doggie toothbrush or simply a gauze pad wrapped around your index finger. You'll need to hold his head still with one hand, while you brush with the other. Brush each tooth in a circular motion—with the brush held at an angle to the gumline—and scrub the tops, fronts, and sides of each tooth. Be sure to use canine toothpaste; our toothpaste will make dogs sick.

While brushing, look for signs of plaque, tartar, and gum disease. Redness, swelling, bad breath, receding gums, and discolored enamel along the gumline are all red flags. If you notice any of these signs, schedule an appointment with

Grooming Shopping List

Here are the items you need to groom your Lab:

BATHING

- ❏ A dog brush for the coat
- ❏ A handheld spray attachment for your tub
- ❏ Dog shampoo (don't use human shampoo)
- ❏ Towels (a chamois is best)
- ❏ A pet hair dryer (you can use your own, but set it on low heat)
- ❏ Spritz-on dry shampoo (handy in case you need a quick clean-up to get rid of dirt or odor)

TRIMMING NAILS

- ❏ Dog nail cutters
- ❏ Nail file or Dremel tool (to file down jagged edges)
- ❏ Styptic stick (in case you cut the quick)

BRUSHING TEETH

- ❏ Dog toothbrush
- ❏ Dog toothpaste (don't use human toothpaste)

CLEANING EARS

- ❏ Cotton balls or wipes
- ❏ Ear-cleaning solution

What's That in His Ear?

Sometimes when dogs play outdoors, they get stuff in their ears, such as seeds, burrs, and foxtails—anything that tends to stick to fur. Check your Labrador Retriever's ears for these things when he comes in from playing outdoors. If left in the ear, they will cause your dog pain and possibly damage his hearing. If you find something and cannot safely remove it at home, take your dog to the vet right away.

your veterinarian. And as a good rule of thumb, most vets suggest you take your dog for yearly dental checkups regardless of his oral health condition.

Nicely Trimmed Nails

Your dog's nails should be trimmed once a month. Be warned that this is one of the least favorite grooming chores for people and for dogs. Puppies naturally do not like pedicures—some of them don't even like for you to touch their paws at all. So as with bathing and teeth care, you need to introduce the idea of nail clipping to your Labrador Retriever puppy as soon as possible.

Try to make the experience as positive as you can. Get out those doggy treats for nail clipping! That way, your puppy will learn that, when you touch his paws or trim those nails, he will get a great food reward. Yum!

At first, hold your Lab's paw in your hand, letting him get used to the idea that you will be holding his paws from time to time. Offer your Lab praise and a treat. Once he seems somewhat comfortable with that, you can start trimming his nails. At first, do only one or two nails at a time. And don't trim a lot of the nail, just nip off the tip or clip at the curved part. It is better to trim a small amount of nail more frequently than to try to cut back a nail that has grown too long.

Long nails can pose a danger to your Lab, making it difficult for him to walk. They can also be painful for you, unintentionally scratching you to shreds while cuddling and playing. Long nails also run the risk of cutting into your dog's footpads, which can be painful and difficult to heal. They also have a greater possibility of snagging on things, causing the nails to rip and bleed. And they can cause the dog's feet to spread. But how do you know when it's time for a pedicure? If you can hear your dog's nails clicking on the floor as he walks around, that's a good indication that his nails are too long.

Hold your Lab still as you trim, taking each paw into your hands and quickly clipping each nail in one movement. Speak soothingly and pet your Lab as you go, trying to keep your dog calm. Guillotine- and scissor-type clippers are the most popular. Be careful not to cut the quick (the pink vein in the nail) as you go; it's very painful, and the nail may bleed profusely. The quick runs partway down into each one of your dog's nails. It's easier to avoid cutting the quick if your dog has light-colored nails because you can see where the vein ends. But unless you have X-ray vision, you're not going to be able to see the veins in dark nails. That's why you need to be extra careful when you trim your dog's nails. If you happen to snip the quick, you can stanch the bleeding with a few drops of a clotting solution or a styptic stick. Once you've cut the nails to the length you want, use a nail file to smooth out any rough edges so they don't catch and rip on anything. Your veterinarian can teach you how to trim your Labrador Retriever's nails properly, or you can schedule regular visits to a groomer.

Keep grooming sessions calm and quiet, and your Labrador Retriever will look forward to this time you spend together.

Good Hearing

Weekly ear checks are a must; you must do them if you want a healthy Labrador Retriever. Those cute floppy Labrador ears can stop airflow and keep the ear canals moist. And nasty stuff tends to grow in moist areas. Some dogs, like people, tend to build up more ear wax than others. Regular cleaning with a specially formulated ear wash from your veterinarian will keep your dog's ears clean and odor-free. Ear cleaning is especially important to do after your dog goes swimming, which Labs love to do. Use a cotton ball or wipe to clean the folds of the upper ear, but do not push it inside because you might damage the eardrum. You can trim any excess hair inside the ear if your Lab will let you.

Symptoms of ear infection include redness and/or swelling of the ear flap or inner ear, a nasty odor, or a dark and waxy discharge. The odor is a common sign of mite infestation. If your Lab digs at his ears, shakes his head a lot, or appears to lose his balance (which can happen with ear problems), see your veterinarian right away.

Labrador Retrievers thoroughly enjoy their time outdoors, which requires more grooming and checks for ticks, mites, and other unwanted pest hitchhikers.

Skunk!

Because Labradors love the great outdoors, part of your job as a responsible Lab owner will be to watch out for any dangers that lurk in the great outdoors. Skunks rank pretty high on many owners' lists of concerns. But if your dog is sprayed, have no fear. While the whole ordeal certainly isn't pleasant, it's not the worst thing in the world.

There will be no mistaking the pungent aroma left lingering after a Labrador's chance encounter with a skunk. If your dog has the misfortune of being sprayed, your first task (and an unpleasant one, at that, to be sure) will be to make sure your dog is physically unharmed. Next, assess where on the body that your dog was sprayed the most. If it's in his eyes or nose, you'll need to head straight for a veterinarian. And if you suspect your Lab has been scratched, he'll need to be up-to-date on his rabies shot.

If you're simply contending with the smell, try this remedy: Combine 1 quart of 3 percent peroxide, with ¼ cup of baking soda, and 1 teaspoon of liquid soap. Mix the ingredients together and watch for it to fizz. Then soak it all over your Labrador's fur, avoiding his eyes. Massage the mixture all over, rinse and repeat as necessary. Follow it up with a regular bath, and the smell should abate.

At a Glance ...

The Labrador Retriever does not need as much grooming as other breeds, but he still needs regular care of his coat, ears, nails, and teeth.

．．

Start grooming when your Lab is a pup so that he doesn't resist grooming as an adult.

．．

To keep his coat super sheen, the Lab's short double coat only needs regular brushing once a week and bathing once or twice a month or as the need arises.

．．

Make tooth brushing part of your Labrador's weekly grooming sessions.

CHAPTER TEN

Healthy Habits

Most Labrador Retrievers typically live for ten to thirteen years. If you want your Lab to be healthy and happy throughout his life, it's important to make sure he eats the right foods, gets plenty of exercise, is groomed regularly, and makes regular visits to the veterinarian. You should know your Lab well enough that you notice when he isn't feeling well right away.

Although a dog should be checked by the breeder's veterinarian before you complete the purchase, you should still take the pup to your own vet as soon as you bring him home. It gives your veterinarian an early start on your own health-care plan for your pet.

Your Lab and His Vet

A good, trustworthy and reliable veterinarian is the most important partner in keeping your Lab healthy. Find a good vet before you bring your puppy home. Ask your friends and family, or check with the local kennel club and your dog's breeder for vets they recommend. A good vet will be happy to answer all your questions and will help you plan your puppy's health care at home.

Take your puppy to the vet within three or four days after you bring him home. If possible, stop by your vet's office after you first pick up your dog, so he

CORE Vaccines
Check with your vet, but all puppies should receive vaccines for the following diseases.

CONDITION	TREATMENT	PROGNOSIS	VACCINE NEEDED
ADENOVIRUS-2 (immunizes against Adenovirus-1, the agent of infectious canine hepatitis)	No curative therapy for infectious hepatitis; treatment geared toward minimizing neurologic effects, shock, hemorrhage, secondary infections	Self-limiting but cross-protects against infectious hepatitis, which is highly contagious and can be mild to rapidly fatal	Recommended
DISTEMPER	No specific treatment; supportive treatment (IV fluids, antibiotics)	High mortality rates	Highly recommended
PARVOVIRUS-2	No specific treatment; supportive treatment (IV fluids, antibiotics)	Highly contagious to young puppies; high mortality rates	Highly recommended
RABIES	No treatment	Fatal	Required

can meet the staff, who will pet and coo over him. This way, your Lab will think the office is a great place to go in the future, rather than a place to fear.

Show the vet all the health records and documents that your breeder gave you when you bought your puppy. He will then check your pup and give him a physical exam to be sure that your Lab is healthy. A good vet will be gentle with your Lab and will try not to frighten the pup. Your vet will also schedule your puppy's first vaccinations.

Many veterinarians have different opinions about which vaccines are best for your puppy, but most recommend about three different shots given every three to four weeks after you bring your puppy in for his first check-up. Your puppy should have had his first set of shots before he left his breeder. Next, your veterinarian will decide which vaccines are best for your dog based on where you live and what risks your puppy will face.

Always ask the veterinarian what shots or medications your dog is getting each time he goes in for a checkup, and ask what the vaccines are for. The more you and your family know about your dog, the better prepared you will be to raise a healthy Labrador Retriever. Keep a notebook or dog diary on your pet's behavior and record all health information, especially after every veterinary visit. It will help you to keep track of any disconcerting new behaviors or bring to attention any odd health or behavioral patterns.

Vac to Basics

The American Veterinary Medical Association (AVMA) recommends certain CORE vaccines for your puppy. These vaccines protect your Labrador Retriever from diseases that are very dangerous to your puppy, such as canine hepatitis and rabies. Many of these CORE vaccines are mandatory in certain states. The rabies vaccine, for example, is required in all fifty states. Your vet will tell you which vaccinations your puppy needs. You can read more about vaccines on the AVMA website, www.avma.org.

So your Labrador loves to swim? Let him! Just be sure to groom him afterward and thoroughly clean and dry his ears to avoid bacterial growth and infection.

During your dog's annual checkups, your vet will give your Lab a general exam and look him over for any health problems. The vet will also ask if you have noticed anything different about your Lab in the past year. Bring your notes on your Lab's behavior with you, and don't be embarrassed to ask any questions about your dog's behavior. There really is no such thing as a dumb question when it comes to your pet's well-being.

What You Can Do

Although most health issues should be taken care of by your dog's veterinarian, there are plenty of things that you can do to keep you Labrador healthy. Keeping him slim and trim, making sure he is groomed and keeping nasty parasites (aka fleas and ticks) off of him are a good start.

Weight Watcher: All Labrador Retrievers love to eat, and they would eat all day long if you let them. But a fat Lab is nothing to laugh about. To make sure your dog isn't overweight, put your hands on his chest. You should be able to

Other Vaccines and Treatment

Depending on where you live and your dog's needs, the following ailments and diseases can be treated through your veterinarian.

CONDITION	TREATMENT	PROGNOSIS	RECOMMENDATION
BORDETELLA (KENNEL COUGH)	Keep warm; humidify room; moderate exercise	Highly contagious; rarely fatal in healthy dogs; easily treated	Optional vaccine; prevalence varies; vaccine may be linked to acute reactions; low efficacy
FLEA AND TICK INFESTATION	Topical and ingestible	Highly contagious	Preventive treatment highly recommended
HEARTWORM	Arsenical compound; rest; restricted exercise	Widely occurring infections; regional preventive programs; successful treatment after early detection	Preventive treatment highly recommended
INTESTINAL WORMS	Dewormer; home medication regimen	Good with prompt treatment	Preventive treatment highly recommended
LYME DISEASE (BORRELIOSIS)	Antibiotics	Can't completely eliminate the organism, but can be controlled in most cases	Vaccine recommended only for dogs with high risk of exposure to deer ticks
PARAINFLUENZA	Rest; humidify room; moderate exercise	Highly contagious; mild; self-limiting; rarely fatal	Optional but recommended; doesn't block infection, but lessens clinical signs
PERIODONTITIS	Dental cleaning; extractions; repair	Excellent, but involves anesthesia	Preventive treatment recommended

feel his ribs through his chest muscles by pressing lightly against his skin with your fingertips; you should not feel a big wad of fat. He should have a thin waistline, and his stomach should rise toward his legs. Just like with people, it's important for your Labrador to be in shape. If your dog is overweight, it can shorten his life.

How can you help your dog stay in shape? First off, do not feed your Lab from your plate. Table scraps aren't healthy for your dog, and they will cause him to gain weight very quickly. It's best to feed your Lab only food and treats made especially for dogs. Keep a record of his weight every year when you take him to the vet. Is your dog gaining weight each year? Then start feeding him a little less, or switch to a low-calorie food. Start taking him on longer walks; it's good for you and your dog!

Coat Check: When you brush your Labrador, check his body for lumps, dry skin, or any other abnormalities. Pay special attention to dry skin and thinning hair, which can be signs of more serious health problems. Check for fleas and flea dirt, especially on your dog's belly and around his tail. Fleas are not only uncomfortable for your dog, but they also can make him sick if not treated (more about that later). If you notice any weird-shaped moles or lumps under your Lab's skin that weren't there before, call the vet.

Eye Spy: Just like for people, your Labrador Retriever's vision may get worse as he gets older. Your Lab's eyes should always be clear and shiny, regardless of his age. If your dog's eyes start to get hazy or cloudy, have your veterinarian take a look.

Keep an eye on your dog's eye health. Periodically check your Lab's eyes for clarity and shine. Hazy, cloudy eyes require a visit to the vet.

No Butts about It: Don't forget your dog's behind! Does he chew at his hind end or scoot around on the carpet? If so, he may have a problem with his

A PIECE OF HISTORY

The original Lab breed died out in Newfoundland because of a heavy dog tax and quarantine law. Many Labs were interbred with other types of retrievers, but luckily the breed prevailed.

anal glands. Your veterinarian or a groomer will be able to release and clean out your Lab's glands (called "expressing the glands"). It's not a job for beginners! Your vet will also ask you to bring in samples of your dog's poop to check for parasites and worms. When you are picking up after your dog each week, check his poop for any signs of parasites (typically small, white worms the size of a grain of rice). Be sure that your dog doesn't have diarrhea or isn't throwing up in the backyard. These are signs that something may be wrong with your Lab's diet or digestion.

Fleas: Fleas have been around for centuries, and they have always caused trouble for dogs and other pets. Not only do the fleas cause your dog to bite and scratch himself, sometimes relentlessly, but they can also cause diseases in your Lab. Chances are your Labrador will get fleas at some point in his life, if not multiple times; it's difficult to avoid since Labs to spend so much time outdoors (and fleas love to spend so much time on dogs)! This is probably the most widely known and thoroughly dreaded frustration in dog ownership. Luckily, there are many ways to fight fleas. A flea infestation may be difficult to prevent, but it's relatively simple to cure.

Because fleas travel on and off their hosts, you'll need to treat both your dog and your home to get rid of them. The most effective method of flea control is a two-stage approach: first kill the adult fleas, then control the development of pre-adult fleas. Treat your home with an insect growth regulator spray and an insecticide to kill the adult fleas. Be sure to cover all carpets, furniture, bedding, pet hang-out areas, and hidden crevices throughout the house.

With topical treatments that you can get from your vet or pet store, fighting fleas is relatively easy. Common treatments available require monthly applications between the shoulder blades and along the dog's back.

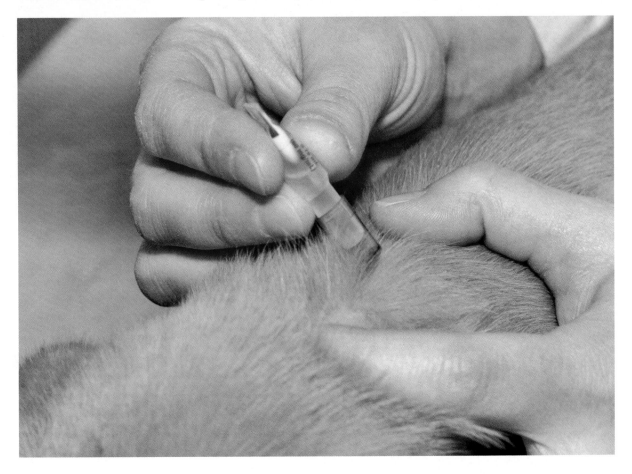

Once you've taken care of your home, you will then need to rid your dog of the fleas traveling on his back. Some products are liquid treatments that you squeeze onto your Labrador's back between his shoulders; others are pills that you give to your dog with his food each month. Alternatively, there are drops available that, when placed on the back of the dog's neck, spread throughout the hair and skin to kill the adult fleas. It is best to ask your veterinarian which medicines are the best to fight your dog's fleas. You can purchase the flea remedies from your veterinarian or from pet stores.

Ticks: Ticks are problematic for dogs because they can spread diseases to your Lab; the most notable of these diseases is Lyme disease (*borreliosis*). These diseases sometimes spread to humans, too. If you live in a place where there are ticks, ask your veterinarian how to protect your dog and if the Lyme disease vaccine is in your dog's best interest.

First Aid

Keeping your Labrador Retriever healthy is a matter of keen observation and quick action when necessary. Knowing your dog's normal behaviors and bodily functions will help you to recognize signs of trouble before they become full-blown emergency situations.

Even if the problem is minor, such as a cut or scrape, it's best to care for the problem immediately to prevent infection, as well as to ensure that your Lab doesn't make the problem worse by chewing or scratching at it. When caring for a wound, remove any splinters or debris, clean with saline solution or warm water, and apply an antibiotic ointment. Bandage the wound if it is on the paw, which can pick up dirt while your dog walks around. It the cut is deep, it may require stitches and should only be treated by a veterinarian.

Consider putting together a basic emergency first aid kit for your dog. Important items to gather include:

- assorted sterile bandages and dressings (including rolls of gauze, which can also be used for a makeshift muzzle)
- an antihistamine (to counteract possible allergic reactions)
- blankets and towels
- disinfectant solution (for flushing out wounds)
- electrolyte solution (for severe dehydration)
- first-aid tape
- ice packs
- name and number of the nearest pet emergency clinic
- a penlight or tiny flashlight
- rolls of sterile cotton
- rubbing alcohol
- scissors (both large and small, blunt-tipped bandage scissors)
- splinting materials
- sterile eye wash or artificial tears
- stethoscope
- thermometer
- tweezers

In an Emergency

While things other than general maintenance should be left to veterinarians, every dog owner should know what to do in case of a canine emergency. Many animal shelters and humane societies have first-aid classes that dog owners can take to learn how to recognize the symptoms of an emergency, how to treat minor injuries, and much more.

The best thing to remember is to know your Lab and his habits. The earlier you realize that something is wrong with your dog, the better chance your vet has of helping him. By checking over your dog's body each week and watching for changes in his behavior, you will be able to let your vet know when there is something wrong with your Lab. Keep your vet's emergency phone number on your refrigerator or by your phone so that he or she can be contacted right away if an emergency occurs.

Support Canine Health Research

The American Kennel Club Canine Health Foundation (AKC CHF) raises money to support canine health research. The foundation makes grants to fund:

- **Identifying the cause(s) of disease**
- **Earlier, more accurate diagnosis**
- **Developing screening tests for breeders**
- **Accurate, positive prognosis**
- **Effective, efficient treatment**

The AKC CHF also supports educational programs that bring scientists together to discuss their work and develop new collaborations to further advance canine health.

The AKC created the AKC CHF in 1995 to raise funds to support canine health research. Each year, the AKC CHF allocates $1.5 million to new canine health research projects.

How You Can Help: If you have an AKC-registered dog, submit his DNA sample (cheek swab or blood sample) to the Canine Health Information Center (CHIC) DNA databank (www.caninehealthinfo.org). Encourage regular health testing by breeders, get involved with your local dog club, and support the efforts to host health education programs. And, if possible, make a donation.

For information, contact the AKC Canine Health Foundation, P.O. Box 900061, Raleigh, NC 27675-9061 or check out the website at www.akcchf.org.

If you notice your Lab is getting chubby, first check with your vet that nothing is seriously wrong. Then amp up your play times together and get him moving. It's great exercise for you both.

At a Glance ...

Find a veterinarian near your home and have an appointment set up before bringing your Labrador Retriever puppy home.

· ·

At your first visit, your vet will set up your puppy's vaccination schedule. Ask your vet which vaccinations are best for your dog.

· ·

Use grooming sessions and regular petting and cuddling as opportunities to check your dog's coat and skin for any problems.

· ·

Be prepared for doggy emergencies by attending a pet first-aid class, having a dog first-aid kit, and keeping your vet's number on the refrigerator or by the phone.

· ·

Be sure to protect your dog from fleas and ticks.

· ·

Know your Lab! Watch your dog for changes in his body and behavior, and call your vet right away if you notice anything different or out of the ordinary.

CHAPTER ELEVEN

An Active Lab is a Healthy Lab

The snoozing, lazy Labrador Retriever in your living room may look content, but in reality he has the energy of an athlete coursing through his body. Given half a chance, he will leap into action!

Labs were originally bred to be hunters, racing across the field to retrieve fallen game birds, brought down by their owners, on land and in the water. Even though the twenty-first century Lab is more pet than hunter, he still hears the

Obedience is a sport enjoyed by dogs and people of all ages. Teaching your dog basic cues is the foundation for all dog training.

same call to action that his ancestors did and needs vigorous exercise and challenging activities to channel all of that energy.

Walking Does Wonders

Although dogs need and want lots of exercise, neither the Lab puppy nor the Lab adult will get enough on his own. You have to provide it for him. A brisk daily walk or (better yet) two walks a day, will help keep your Labrador Retriever fit and trim. It also will keep your dog's mind alert, as he takes in the sights and sounds of street life or the neighborhood park while you walk.

How long and how far should you walk your Lab? The answers to those questions depend on your dog's age, his physical condition, and his energy level. Take it easier with a puppy that is younger than a year old; his bones are softer than those of an adult Lab, so he's more likely to get injured if too much stress is put on his body. Until your puppy is a year old, you need to take shorter walks and stay away from playing games with him that encourage jumping or heavy impact on his front or rear. Playtime with other puppies and older dogs should be supervised to avoid excessive wrestling and twisting until your pup has celebrated his first birthday.

When and where should you take your Lab for a walk? On warm days, avoid the heat by walking him during the cooler morning or evening hours. It'll be a great time for the two of you to bond, too. Your Lab will eagerly look forward

Just for Tweens and Teens

The American Kennel Club has a whole program dedicated to Junior Showmanship for kids between nine and eighteen years old who are interested in handling and showing their dogs at dog shows and dog handling competitions. As a Junior Handler, you will take classes about dog shows and competitions including obedience, agility, tracking, and rally. If you think your Lab is good enough to compete with other Labs at dog shows and training competitions, enroll in the Junior Showmanship program and really show off your best friend! Learn more at www.akc.org/kids_juniors. The Labrador Retriever Club sponsors a Junior Showmanship Incentive Program. Check it out at www.thelabradorclub .com, click Programs then Junior Showmanship.

Hold off on strenuous exercise and competition until your Lab is a year old. Give his bones, joints, and muscles a chance to fully develop.

to these special times with you. As a creature of habit, your dog will eventually become excited when he sees you pick up his leash.

Head of the Class

Beyond the everyday exercise options of walking and playing, your Labrador Retriever might enjoy spending time with other people and dogs in competitive canine sports. From agility to conformation to field hunting trials, many dogs enjoy sports that test their smarts and athletic prowess. If this sounds like something you and your dog would enjoy, there are many ways to get involved.

Puppies aren't allowed in competition because they aren't done growing, but once your Lab turns a year old, he should be ready for the game. However, before you start any type of strenuous exercise, consult your veterinarian to make sure your dog is healthy enough to participate.

Start with classes in a specific sport. If your Lab shows a talent for agility, obedience, or hunting trials, consider competing. The American Kennel Club and the Labrador Retriever Club (the Labrador parent club) offer competition outlets for all sports listed below. To compete in these events, you must have a dog registered with the AKC. Shows and trials are held year-round and are designed for all levels of experience.

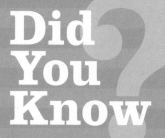

Did You Know?

The Labrador Retriever has been the most popular dog breed in the United States since 1991. For more than 20 years, more Labradors have been registered with the AKC each year than any other breed.

Obedience

In obedience training, a pup learns to follow basic cues (*sit*, *down*, *stay*, *come*, etc.), and you learn how to properly give those cues. Plan a weekly night out with your Labrador by enrolling him in a class. The benefits of obedience classes are endless. You'll both be more active and healthier. Your dog will learn the basics of obedience, be better behaved, and become a model canine citizen. (See page 75 for information about the AKC Canine Good Citizen Program.) As an added benefit, he will discover that you really are his leader! Special puppy obedience classes are available, too.

Is your dog a whiz in training classes? If so, you may be ready to take the next step and enter an obedience practice match or show in the beginner novice class at an obedience trial, which tests dogs to see how well they behave. But more than that, AKC obedience trials demonstrate the usefulness of dogs as companions to humans. Developed in the 1930s, it is one of the AKC's oldest events. Obedience trials showcase dogs that have been trained and conditioned to behave well in the home, in public places, and in the presence of other dogs. The sport offers different levels of competition and is great for owners and dogs who prefer to compete against themselves. Learn all about the AKC's obedience program, the sport's history, its importance, and the obedience titles that you and your dog can earn at www.akc.org/events/obedience.

Agility

If your Labrador loves to run and jump—and what Lab doesn't?—then agility is the sport for you! Running a dog in an agility trial is the ultimate game for you and your dog, and it is one of the most exciting canine sports for spectators. Lots of Labradors love agility, a timed obstacle-course sport created just for dogs. In an agility

Agility competitions feature obstacle courses full of fun toys. The timed events provide great exercise for the energetic Labrador Retriever.

trial, the dog demonstrates his agile nature and versatility by following cues from his handler while maneuvering through jumps, tunnels, weave poles, and other objects. It's an activity that strengthens the bond between dog and handler and provides fun and exercise for both, which might explain why it's so enjoyable to watch!

But you can't just show up and enter an event. Your Lab must first learn how to negotiate the obstacles and follow your cues correctly. To do this, you need to enroll your dog in an agility class. In agility, your dog will learn to climb an A-frame ramp, race headlong through a tunnel, balance himself on a teeter-totter, jump onto and off of a platform, jump through a hoop, zigzag between a row of posts, and much more! He'll expend energy, and you will be bursting with pride as he masters each task.

Although puppies aren't allowed to begin training until they are a year old, you can begin socializing your dog to the equipment by letting him sniff around the course and by placing him on the objects and petting him while he is in place. Learn more about AKC's agility events at www.akc.org/events/agility.

Dog Shows

The original canine competition for all breeds is conformation (a.k.a. entering a dog show), and Labrador Retrievers are popular choices at shows around the country. At a dog show, your Lab will be examined by a judge to see how well he conforms to the breed standard (a written, physical description of how the perfect Labrador Retriever should look and act). If your dog is AKC-registerd and you want to try your hand at dog shows, there are events in your community called match or canine experience shows, which are developed especially for first-time exhibitors and their dogs to get their paws wet in the show ring.

Before you involve your Labrador in any dog shows, take him for his ACK Canine Good Citizen testing. Receiving the certification will prove he's ready to face the rigors of the championship ring.

Labs are great hunting partners. Their keen eyesight and sense of smell help them retrieve gamebirds.

If you plan to show your Labrador, make sure you look for a show-quality puppy and discuss your goals with the breeder. Your Lab will need to be unaltered (not spayed or neutered). Many local clubs host conformation training classes and can help beginners get started with their pups.

The AKC's website has extensive information on conformation—check out www.akc.org/events/conformation/beginners.cfm for newcomer information. Then make your introduction in the show ring by finding a match or canine experience show near you at www.akc.org/public_education/education_match.cfm.

Rally

If you're looking for an activity that combines the precision of obedience with the fast-paced style of agility, then try the newest AKC sport—rally. Rally was developed after rally-style auto racing. In rally, the dog/handler team must navigate a course made up of directional signs. Each course is unique, keeping competitors on their toes. It's great for first-time competitors or anyone new to companion events.

If you choose to compete as your dog's handler, you and your Lab will get to show off your skills together. Like in obedience trials, you show how well your dog does what you ask him to. But the performance rules for rally aren't as strict as those for obedience, so you can be more relaxed and have more fun! Side by side, you and your Lab will work your way through a rally course, which has ten to twenty stations. At each station, you and your Labrador Retriever are asked to show off some skill. For more information on rally competitions, log on to www.akc.org/events/rally.

Hunting Tests

Labradors who enter hunting tests are judged on their hunting abilities, especially their ability to retrieve (find and bring back killed birds, like pheasants or ducks, to their owners on land or in the water). Your Lab won't be competing against other dogs for a win. His hunting skills will just be judged against a standard of performance. A Labrador's love of "bird work" can range from mild to wildly passionate, but almost every Lab will enjoy working in the field. The AKC has hunting tests especially for retrievers. Go online to www.akc.org/events/hunting_tests/retrievers.

Field Trials

Like in hunting tests, Labs competing in field trials are judged on their hunting abilities. The difference is that, in field trials, Labs have to compete against each other for a win. The field trials are considered the most challenging and difficult of all sporting dog events, and Labs—no surprise to their proud owners—earn more field championships every year than any other breed. As field dogs, no breed outdoes the Labrador! Go to www.akc.org/events/field_trials/retrievers to learn more about AKC retriever field trials.

Tracking

Have you ever seen a movie in which a dog is sent out to find a lost person? What the dog is doing is called tracking. In competitive tracking events, dogs show off their natural ability to follow the scent of a particular person. It's great exercise for your Labrador Retriever and another chance for the two of you to work together while having fun. Log on to www.akc.org/events/tracking for information about the AKC's tracking events.

Dock Diving

Dock diving (also known as dock jumping) is a relatively new dog sport in which dogs compete against each other in jumping into a body of water from a dock. The dogs are judged for distance and height. If this sounds like a sport your Lab

Labs have been jumping off docks for years. Now there's a sport geared toward this very activity. Dock diving is fun for dogs and even more fun to watch.

Dock diving lends well to the Labrador's build and love of swimming. The new sport has amassed great popularity in the past ten years.

would love, check out the following sanctioned organizations for information on how to get involved:

- **DockDogs:** DockDogs' event took place during the ESPN 2000 Great Outdoor Games and gained so much popularity that the organization established its own competition operations by 2002. What started as a six-event program now has more than 150 qualifying events throughout the United States, Canada, and United Kingdom each year. For more information, go to www.dockdogs.com.

- **Splash Dogs:** Started in 2003, Splash Dogs organizes and promotes dock jumping events across America. The national organization tracks overall event and individual rankings as well as offering a multi-level titling program for all participants. Learn more about the organization at www.splashdogs.com.

- **Ultimate Air Dogs:** Founded in 2005 by Major League Baseball player Milt Wilcox, Ultimate Air Dogs first began as a grassroots dock jumping club in Michigan. Now the organization hosts year-round events throughout America. Go to www.ultimateairdogs.net to find out if there is an upcoming event near you.

Working Dogs

Because of their gentle and helpful nature, Labrador Retrievers are a favorite breed for many service professions including, search and rescue, police work, disabled person assistance, and therapy work. Most service dogs are specially chosen from breeders and trained for the job from an early age. However, if you have a willing Lab, you can involve him in therapy work at any time, visiting sick and elderly people in assistance facilities and sharing their unconditional love with those in need. If you think your Lab would be perfect in this line of work, contact the following organizations for more information to get started:

- **AKC's Canine Good Citizen® Program:** Rewarding dogs that have good manners at home and in the community, this two-part program requires dogs to pass a ten-step test to receive a certificate touting the dog's preparedness for positive interaction in your community. Contact the program at www.akc.org/events/cgc.

- **AKC Therapy Dog Title program:** This recognizes all AKC dog and owner teams who have volunteered their time and helped people in therapy work. It awards an official AKC Therapy Dog title (AKC ThD) to dogs that have been certified by recognized therapy dog associations and have worked to improve the lives of the people they have visited. For more information, visit www.akc.org/akctherapydog.

- **Pet Partners®:** This international nonprofit organization matches people with mental and physical disabilities and patients in healthcare facilities together with professionally trained animals to help improve the patients' health. Learn more at www.petpartners.org.

- **Therapy Dogs Inc.:** This organization provides registration, support, and insurance for members who are involved in animal-assisted volunteer activities. Visit www.therapydogs.com for more information.

- **Therapy Dogs International:** This nonprofit volunteer group helps qualified handlers and their therapy dogs visit facilities and institutions where therapy dogs are needed. Go to www.tdi-dog.org to find out how you can get involved.

Your Lab's Favorite Playmate—You!

Competition aside, your Labrador Retriever will be happiest when he is with people, especially his owners. He needs to be part of family activities, he loves to play with the kids, and he will be an eager participant in outdoor sports and indoor play. If any single word befits the Labrador Retriever, it's "family."

Friendly Labs that enjoy meeting new people make for wonderful therapy dogs. Consider this service if you want to share your special pet's love outside of your home.

At a Glance ...

Because Labrador Retrievers have so many natural skills and so much energy, you and your dog have lots of ways to stay active.

. . . .

Your Lab needs at least two good walks each day to stay fit and keep his mind alert.

. . . .

Take an obedience or agility class with your Lab; it's a good way for him to learn some basic commands and for the two of you to have fun.

. . . .

Competing in AKC events can be challenging and fun. Your Labrador will enjoy honing his natural skills in events such as obedience, rally, and agility; hunt and field tests, and tracking.

. . . .

If you have a show-quality pup, you can train for and compete in conformation shows.

Resources

BOOKS

The American Kennel Club's Meet the Breeds: Dog Breeds from A to Z, 2012 edition (Irvine, California: I-5 Press, 2011) The ideal puppy buyer's guide, this book has all you need to know about each breed currently recognized by the AKC.

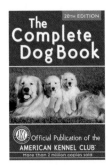

The Complete Dog Book, 20th edition (New York: Ballantine Books, 2006) This official publication of the AKC, first published in 1929, includes the complete histories and breed standards of 153 recognized breeds, as well as information on general care and the dog sport.

The Complete Dog Book for Kids (New York: Howell Book House, 1996) Specifically geared toward young people, this official publication of the AKC presents 149 breeds and varieties, as well as introductory owners' information.

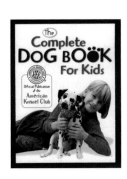

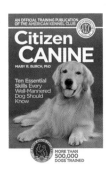

Citizen Canine: Ten Essential Skills Every Well-Mannered Dog Should Know by Mary R. Burch, PhD (Freehold, New Jersey: Kennel Club Books, 2010) This official AKC publication is the definitive guide to the AKC's Canine Good Citizen® Program, recognized as the gold standard of behavior for dogs, with more than half a million dogs trained.

DOGS: The First 125 Years of the American Kennel Club (Freehold, New Jersey: Kennel Club Books, 2009) This official AKC publication presents an authoritative, complete history of the AKC, including detailed information not found in any other volume.

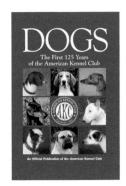

Dog Heroes of September 11th: A Tribute to America's Search and Rescue Dogs, 10th anniversary edition, by Nona Kilgore Bauer (Freehold, New Jersey: Kennel Club Books, 2011) A publication to salute the canines that served in the recovery missions following the September 11th attacks, this book serves as a lasting tribute to these noble American heroes.

The Original Dog Bible: The Definitive Source for All Things Dog, 2nd edition, by Kristin Mehus-Roe (Irvine, California: I-5 Press, 2009) This 831-page magnum opus includes more than 250 breed profiles, hundreds of color photographs, and a wealth of information on every dog topic imaginable—thousands of practical tips on grooming, training, care, and much more.

PERIODICALS

American Kennel Club Gazette

Every month since 1889, serious dog fanciers have looked to the *AKC Gazette* for authoritative advice on training, showing, breeding, and canine health. Each issue

includes the breed columns section, written by experts from the respective breed clubs. Only available electronically.

AKC Family Dog

This is a bimonthly magazine for the dog lover whose special dog is "just a pet." Helpful tips, how-tos, and features are written in an entertaining and reader-friendly format. It's a lifestyle magazine for today's busy families who want to enjoy a rewarding, mutually happy relationship with their canine companions.

Dog Fancy

The world's most widely read dog magazine, *Dog Fancy* celebrates dogs and the people who love them. Each monthly issue includes info on cutting-edge medical developments, health and fitness (with a focus on prevention, treatment, and natural

therapy), behavior and training, travel and activities, breed profiles and dog news, issues and trends for purebred and mixed-breed dog owners. The magazine informs, inspires, and entertains while promoting responsible dog ownership. Throughout its more than forty-year history, *Dog Fancy* has garnered numerous honors, including being named the Best All-Breed Magazine by the Dog Writers Association of America.

Dogs in Review

For more than fifteen years, *Dogs in Review* has showcased the finest dogs in the United States and from around the world. The emphasis has always been on strong content, with input

from distinguished breeders, judges, and handlers worldwide. This global perspective distinguishes this monthly publication from its competitors—no other North American dog-show magazine gathers together so many international experts to enlighten and entertain its readership.

Dog World Annual

Dog World annual is a lifestyle magazine published by the editors of *Dog Fancy* that covers all aspects of the dog world: culture, art, history, travel, sports, and science. It also profiles breeds to help prospective owners choose the best dogs for their future needs, such as a potential show champion, super service dog, great pet, or competitive star.

Natural Dog

Natural Dog is the magazine dedicated to giving a dog a natural lifestyle. From nutritional choices to grooming to dog-supply options, this publication helps readers make the transition from traditional to natural methods. The magazine also explores the array of complementary treatments available for today's dogs:

acupuncture, massage, homeopathy, aromatherapy, and much more. *Natural Dog* is issued as an annual publication and occasionally appears as a special insert section in *Dog Fancy* magazine.

Puppies USA

Also from the editors of *Dog Fancy,* this annual magazine offers essential information for all new puppy owners. *Puppies USA* is lively and informative, including advice on general care, nutrition, grooming, and training techniques for all puppies, whether purebred or mixed breed, adopted, rescued, or purchased. In addition, it offers family fun through quizzes, contests, and much more. An extensive breeder directory is included.

WEBSITES

www.akc.org

The American Kennel Club's (AKC's) website is an excellent starting point for researching dog breeds and learning about puppy care. The site lists hundreds of breeders, along with basic information about breed selection and basic care. The site also has links to the national breed club of every AKC-recognized breed; breed-club sites offer plenty of detailed breed information, as well as lists of member breeders. In addition, you can find the AKC National Breed Club Rescue List at www.akc.org/breeds/rescue.cfm. If looking for purebred puppies, go to www.puppybuyerinfo.com for AKC classifieds and parent-club referrals.

www.dogchannel.com

Powered by *Dog Fancy,* Dog Channel is "the website for dog lovers," where hundreds of thousands of visitors each month find extensive information on breeds, training, health and nutrition, puppies, care, activities, and more. Interactive features include forums, Dog College, games, and Club Dog, a free club where dog lovers can create blogs for their pets and earn points to buy products. DogChannel is the one-stop site for all things dog.

www.meetthebreeds.com

The official website of the AKC Meet the Breeds® event, hosted by the American Kennel Club in the Jacob Javits Center in New York City in the fall. The first Meet the Breeds event took place in 2009. The website includes information on every recognized breed of dog and cat, alphabetically listed, as well as the breeders, demonstration facilitators, sponsors, and vendors participating in the annual event.

AKC AFFILIATES

The **AKC Museum of the Dog**, established in 1981, is located in St. Louis, Missouri, and houses the world's finest collection of art devoted to the dog. Visit www.museumofthedog.org.

The **AKC Humane Fund** promotes the joy and value of responsible and productive pet ownership through education, outreach, and grant-making. Monies raised may fund grants to organizations that teach responsible pet ownership; provide for the health and well-being of all dogs; and preserve and celebrate the human-animal bond and the evolutionary relationship between dogs and humankind. Go to www.akchumanefund.org.

The **American Kennel Club Companion Animal Recovery (CAR) Corporation** is dedicated to reuniting lost microchipped and tattooed pets with their owners. AKC CAR maintains a permanent-identification database and provides lifetime recovery services 24 hours a day, 365 days a year, for all animal species. Millions of pets are enrolled in the program, which was established in 1995. Visit www.akccar.org.

The **American Kennel Club Canine Health Foundation (AKC CHF), Inc.** is the largest foundation in the world to fund canine-only health studies for purebred and mixed-breed dogs. More than $22 million has been allocated in research funds to more than 500 health studies conducted to help dogs live longer, healthier lives. Go to www.akcchf.org.

AKC PROGRAMS

The **Canine Good Citizen Program (CGC)** was established in 1989 and is designed to recognize dogs that have good manners at home and in the community. This rapidly growing, nationally recognized program stresses responsible dog ownership for owners and basic training and good manners for dogs. All dogs that pass the ten-step Canine Good Citizen test receive a certificate from the American Kennel Club. Go to www.akc.org/events/cgc.

The **AKC S.T.A.R. Puppy Program** is designed to get dog owners and their puppies off to a good start and is aimed at loving dog owners who have taken the time to attend basic obedience classes with their puppies. After completing a six-week training course, the puppy must pass the AKC S.T.A.R. Puppy test, which evaluates Socialization, Training, Activity, and Responsibility. Go to www.akc.org/starpuppy.

The **AKC Therapy Dog** program recognizes all American Kennel Club dogs and their owners who have given their time and helped people by volunteering as a therapy dog-and-owner team. The AKC Therapy Dog program is an official American Kennel Club title awarded to dogs that have worked to improve the lives of the people they have visited. The AKC Therapy Dog title (AKC ThD) can be earned by dogs that have been certified by recognized therapy dog organizations. For more information, visit www.akc.org/akctherapydog.

Index

AMERICAN
KENNEL CLUB®

Advocating for the purebred dog as a family companion, advancing canine health and well-being, working to protect the rights of all dog owners and promoting responsible dog ownership, the **American Kennel Club:**

Sponsors more than **22,000 sanctioned events** annually including conformation, agility, obedience, rally, tracking, lure coursing, earthdog, herding, field trial, hunt test, and coonhound events

Features a **10-step Canine Good Citizen® program** that rewards dogs who have good manners at home and in the community

Has reunited more than **400,000** lost pets with their owners through the AKC Companion Animal Recovery - visit **www.akccar.org**

Created and supports the AKC Canine Health Foundation, which funds research projects using the more than **$22 million** the AKC has donated since 1995 - visit **www.akcchf.org**

Joins **animal lovers** through education, outreach and grant-making via the AKC Humane Fund - visit **www.akchumanefund.org**

We're more than champion dogs. We're the dog's champion.

www.akc.org